LET'S MEET THE PROPHETS

By the same author

*Praying the Sunday Psalms: a comprehensive resource
for each liturgical year* (years A, B, and C)

*New Light: Discovering the Psalms in the
Prayer of the Church*

Praying the Prayer of the Church

LET'S MEET THE PROPHETS
speaking for God in critical times

Richard Atherton

A Redemptorist Publication

Copyright © Richard Atherton, 2008

Published by **Redemptorist Publications**
A Registered Charity limited by guarantee.
Registered in England 3261721.

First published September 2008

Layout by Peena Lad
Cover by Chris Nutbeen

Maps on pages 130-131 drawn by Simon Atherton.

ISBN 978-0-85231-353-4

A CIP catalogue record for this book is available from the British Library

Printed by Cambridge University Press

Redemptorist
P U B L I C A T I O N S
Alphonsus House Chawton Hampshire GU34 3HQ
Telephone 01420 88222   Fax 01420 88805
rp@rpbooks.co.uk   www.rpbooks.co.uk

CONTENTS

Preface

In the Creed we proclaim our belief that the Holy Spirit "has spoken through the Prophets", but for many of us these messengers of the Holy Spirit are virtually unknown. I am reminded of a friend of mine who always spends his holidays in the same area. He goes to Mass there each Sunday but, even after many years, apart from the odd nod of recognition and occasional "Good morning", he feels that the local parishioners are still strangers. "Somehow," he explains, "I feel I've never really met them."

Similarly, we have rubbed shoulders, so to say, with the prophets for years; but we are still only on nodding terms, we have never really met. And yet the prophets make up about a quarter of the Old Testament and figure prominently in the Church's liturgy, especially in the Sunday readings and the Prayer of the Church. Moreover, in the words of a modern scholar, "their influence upon the religion of Israel, [and even] upon the whole world, cannot be overestimated".[1]

Admittedly, the prophets do not make for easy reading. Even their names can sometimes sound off-puttingly exotic – Zephaniah, for example, or Nahum or Habakkuk. In fact the books attributed to them are not books, as we understand the term. The prophets were preachers rather than writers, purveyors of the spoken rather than the written word. As a rule, it was their followers who put the books together, after gathering as best they could the various sayings of the prophet. They were not unduly concerned about chronology, and there was always a great deal of editing and emending before the book appeared in its final form.

It's perhaps not without significance, then, that the only time in the whole Bible that an individual seeks guidance in understanding sacred scripture, he is reading one of the prophets. The story, told in Acts 8:26-40, records how an Ethiopian official, on his way home from Jerusalem by chariot, was reading a passage from Isaiah. The deacon Philip overheard him   in those days people read aloud – and asked if he understood what he was reading. "How can I," was the reply, "unless someone guides me?" Philip didn't need further encouragement: soon the two men were sharing the chariot, and, as Philip explained the passage from Isaiah, the Ethiopian discovered "the good news about Jesus". Soon afterwards he was being baptised.

---

[1] John F.A. Sawyer, *Prophecy and the Prophets of the Old Testament* (Oxford: Oxford University Press, 1987), p. 2.

This book is a humble attempt to help those who are looking for someone to guide them in the reading of the prophets. The first chapter offers background information about the meaning of prophecy and about the extraordinary men and women who were called to that ministry. There we shall see that all the prophets who have left books to us lived in or about the most tragic event in Israel's history – the grim years of exile in far-away Babylon. And so the chapters are divided into three sections: "Section One – Before the Exile", "Section Two – The Exile" and "Section Three – After the Exile". We will take the prophets in their chronological order, and since some knowledge of the historical background is highly desirable, if not essential, for a genuine understanding of the prophets, there are several sections ("You are here…") that offer a brief review of the historical background to the prophets who appear in the succeeding pages.

I wish to record my thanks to Fr Tim Swinglehurst for reading through the first manuscript of this book and offering valuable advice, to my nephew Simon for providing the excellent maps, and to the staff at Redemptorist Publications for their expertise and unfailing support.

Naturally, I hope that this book will encourage you to read the prophets – reading them is infinitely more important than reading about them – but above all I hope that in meeting the prophets and growing to know them, we, like the Ethiopian in his chariot, will find ourselves being drawn ever more closely to the One in whom all prophecy is fulfilled – Jesus, the Lord.

Richard Atherton

"God spoke... through the prophets"

When anyone – politician, football manager, even bishop – is asked their view about the future, the reply is likely to begin: "I'm no prophet, but..." In everyday language "prophecy" has become a synonym for fortune-telling. In the Bible, however, prophets are divinely blessed not so much with foresight as with insight; their skill is not primarily in foretelling but in forth-telling: they are God's spokesmen and women. Modern counterparts might be a Pope John, a Martin Luther King or an Oscar Romero. Their supreme task is to uphold the intimate relationship between God and God's people, and this means confronting those whose behaviour threatens the relationship. What they offer is a diagnosis of current ills, though usually with a prognosis of what will happen if people do not respond. Their voices are powerful, challenging, fearless.

There were "false prophets", too, whom Micah wryly describes as ready to proclaim peace so long as you give them "something to eat" but to threaten war if you put "nothing into their mouths" (3:5). However, over time genuine prophets came to be recognised as such: what they said rang true, it was in accord with the tradition of the community. And so their authority came to be regarded as similar to that of the Law; the phrase "the Law and the Prophets" became a consecrated expression for the totality of God's revelation in the Old Testament (cf. Matthew 7:12; 11:13; 22:40).

There were many prophets in Israel's history, stretching from the days of the Exodus in the thirteenth century BC until long after the return from exile in the sixth century BC. Some, like Isaiah, were permanent court prophets, the king's men, though always ready to confront him; others, like Amos, claimed they were not professional prophets at all – they kept their day job. Others worked in associations or guilds, the ecstatic behaviour of these "sons of prophets" often bordering on the frenetic. But one group of prophets stands apart from the rest and is our concern in this book. Often called the "classical" prophets, they are unique in having biblical books named after them (Amos, Hosea, Ezekiel and so on). They are the first prophets of whose preaching we have a written record, though that record was compiled, often with emendations, by their followers. Four of them – Isaiah, Jeremiah, Ezekiel and Daniel – are known as "major prophets" because of the length of their books, the other twelve as "minor prophets".

"In many and various ways…"

If, as the Letter to the Hebrews says in its opening sentence, it was in "many and various ways" that God "spoke by the prophets", the variety was due in part to the diversity of personalities involved. The prophets were flesh-and-blood creatures like ourselves, with hopes and anxieties, loves and animosities, joys and fears; they had to earn their living, some had families to look after, they lived by faith, they were influenced by what was happening in their world, they were sometimes depressed and disheartened. The word of God was filtered through their experiences and personalities: so that the language of the courtly Isaiah is not that of Amos the hardy shepherd; the experiences of Hosea, who had to cope with an unfaithful wife, are not those of Ezekiel the Temple priest whose wife was "the delight of [his] eyes".

Unfortunately our knowledge of their lives and personal traits is extremely limited, and yet, as they would be the first to insist, the prophetic message is infinitely more important than the messengers who proclaim it. Moreover, despite many differences, they have much in common. All work out of the conviction that God has charged them with a mission; in many cases it was some type of mystical experience that launched them on their prophetic career. They know that they speak in God's name and with God's authority, a conviction articulated by the expression "Thus says the Lord". They display courage, sometimes heroism: being a prophet is a lonely and even dangerous profession; the prophet will be largely ignored, often have to face hostility. Jesus would speak of the treatment typically meted out to prophets: "Jerusalem, Jerusalem, the city that kills the prophets and stones those who are sent to it!" (Matthew 23:37).

The prophets are united in their belief that the Lord is Lord of history, that the superpowers of the day are in his control (even if it does not always seem so) and that he will never finally abandon his people. They are united also in accepting that the covenant is at the heart of Israel's faith and of their own mission. They see themselves not as innovators but as guardians of tradition. Just as the aim of the Second Vatican Council was not to teach new truths but to bring to light what had been neglected, or to present "old" ones in ways that speak to today, so the prophets are at one in the conviction that they offer not a new message but a new awareness of the traditional faith; and their common plea is that that faith will influence the people's lives at a personal, national and international level.

In all their difficulties, they find strength in the history of their people, recalling how the Lord rescued them from slavery in Egypt, fashioned them during the years of trekking through the desert, entered into a covenant with them so that henceforth he would be their God and they his people, and finally led them to their Promised Land of Canaan. As they began to establish themselves, they realised the need for a king and David was the answer to their dreams. With his coronation (c.1000 BC) a golden age seemed to have dawned. He captured Jerusalem, making it his capital, and had the ark of the covenant brought there, so that Jerusalem became both the political and the spiritual heart of the nation. Under his successor, Solomon, a magnificent Temple was raised to house the ark and be the tangible sign that the Lord was in the midst of his people.

However, there was a darker side to Israel's history. Being God's people brought with it moral obligations, and the prophets interpreted the tragedies that befell Israel as punishment for their betrayals. One of the greatest tragedies occurred after Solomon's death (922 BC): the ten northern tribes and the two southern went their separate ways, a schism that was never healed. Palestine was a bridge between two major powers, Mesopotamia (Assyria and Babylon) to the north and Egypt to the south. While the people benefited from merchants who travelled up and down the bridge with their wares, they also suffered from the trampling feet of soldiers over that same bridge. They were seldom left in peace; there were threats and invasions, they saw the northern kingdom wiped off the map and the southerners taken into exile. And even when exile was over, further troubles awaited them, culminating in the persecution of those who refused to comply with the policy of "hellenisation" inaugurated by Alexander the Great, who wanted to see the universal acceptance of Greek customs and culture.

Time and again, God raised up prophets to support the people, now encouraging them with promises of a glorious future, now chiding them for their infidelities, but always assuring them of the Lord's unchanging faithfulness. Tirelessly, they warned against the abiding temptations: that of combining pagan rituals with worship of God; that of trusting in armaments and military alliances rather than in the Lord; and that of seeking wealth at the cost of justice to the poor. If the "many and various ways" God spoke through the prophets was due in part to the contrasting personalities of the prophets, it was also due to the various political, religious and social upheavals which God's people encountered during some of the most turbulent years of Israel's history.

"In these last days he has spoken to us by a Son"

The struggles of these ancient people and the books written by them more than two thousand years ago might seem irrelevant in the third millennium. And yet, as part of the inspired word of God, the message of the prophets has intrinsic value and a lasting religious significance. The prophetic books contain poetry that compares favourably with that of the psalms; and, like the psalms, this poetry features generously in the Church's liturgy.

The Gospel writers are at pains to show how Jesus is the key to the scriptures, and in particular to the utterances of the prophets. Of course Old Testament passages are not "photographic anticipations of future events";[1] the prophets were addressing the people of their own day and their words "had an immediate import and meaning for their contemporaries". However, they are often found to have "a fuller meaning", "a surplus of meaning", revealed by the rereading of the ancient texts through Christian eyes; this discovery of an additional layer of meaning in the text is made possible only in the light of the life, death and resurrection of Jesus and the guidance of the Spirit. St Augustine comments: "The Church has heard the promises that were made, she sees their fulfilment; she has heard in the prophecies, she sees in the gospel" (on Psalm 47).

The Gospels present Jesus at his transfiguration flanked by Moses and Elijah, as if to say: here is the fulfilment not only of the Law (Moses) but also of the prophets (Elijah). In more than a dozen places he is given the title of prophet. After the feeding of the five thousand, people said: "This is indeed the prophet who is to come into the world" (John 6:14). Similarly, the disciples told Jesus that people believed him to be "one of the prophets" (Mark 8:28). As he heads for Jerusalem, he insists: "it is impossible for a prophet to be killed outside of Jerusalem" (Luke 13:33). And after hearing his parable of the vineyard, the chief priests and the Pharisees "wanted to arrest him, but they feared the crowds, because they regarded him as a prophet" (Matthew 21:46). The two disciples travelling to Emmaus early on Easter Sunday morning spoke of him as "a prophet mighty in deed and word" (Luke 24:19); and Jesus, "beginning with Moses and all the prophets... interpreted to them the things about himself in all the scriptures" (Luke 24:27). In the Acts of the Apostles, Peter explains that the curing of a lame man is attributable to Jesus, who is the fulfilment of Moses' ancient promise that "The Lord your God will raise up for you from your own people a prophet like me" (Acts 3:22; Deuteronomy 18:15. 18). There is a sense, then, in which Jesus is the supreme prophet, *the* spokesman of God, "*the* Word [of God] made flesh", both divine messenger and divine message. But, in another sense, he is much more. As he once told his hearers: "something greater than Jonah [or any other prophet] is here!" (Matthew 12:41).

---

[1] Quotes in this paragraph from the Pontifical Biblical Commission, *The Jewish People and their Sacred Scriptures in the Christian Bible* (Vatican: Libreria editrice vaticana, 2002).

The fact that God has spoken to us uniquely through his Son does not lead us to ignore the prophets; on the contrary, the prophetic books are of supreme value because, in the words of the fourth Eucharistic Prayer, "through the prophets [God] taught [us] to hope for salvation": they serve as a preparation for the coming of Jesus, so that our knowledge of them enriches our understanding of him.

SECTION ONE
Before the Exile

The eighth-century prophets

It's the middle of the eighth century before the birth of Christ. For more than fifty years the nation has been divided into Israel in the north and Judah in the south. They have warred with each other and constantly been under threat from powerful neighbours. On the whole Israel has fared better than Judah, but there is political instability in the north and a constant attempt to combine traditional religion with Canaanite practices. Cut off from easy access to the Temple at Jerusalem, the northerners have shrines of their own. The reign of Jeroboam II (786–746 BC) witnesses an upsurge of trade, military power, building programmes and material prosperity but is accompanied by merciless oppression of the poor.

The time is ripe for the appearance of the first of the classical prophets. AMOS, coming up from Judah, warns Israel of the terrible fate that awaits it from the expanding power of Assyria. A few years later, HOSEA, himself a northerner, raises a similar cry in the north. The threatening words of the prophets are soon to be tragically realised. For a time the northerners delay the inevitable by a series of spoiling tactics – now paying the Assyrians tribute, now making alliances against them, now surrendering to them and, once the threat has passed, plotting against them again. Finally the Assyrians besiege Samaria, capital of the north, and two years later the city falls and the population is scattered throughout the Assyrian empire. The year is 721; the northern kingdom is no more.

Meanwhile, the history of the kingdom of Judah has run its parallel course. Less vulnerable than Israel because of its isolated position and less desirable because of its insignificant size, it has enjoyed periods of prosperity, especially under King Uzziah, whose long reign (783–742) virtually coincided with that of Jeroboam II in the north. But if his reign was peaceful and prosperous, the seeds of spiritual decay, similar to those in the north, are already present and the prophet ISAIAH insists that unless the people return to the Lord, the all-holy One, and rely upon him, their fate will be like that of their northern kinsfolk. At about the same time the prophet MICAH attacks the lack of justice among the people and their failure to reflect in their lives the God they worship.

The threat of Assyrian invasion has hung over the land for some time. When, in 735, Judah refuses to join Israel and Syria in an attempt to stem the Assyrian advance, war is declared on Judah. The southern king, Ahaz, seeks the protection of Assyria, though Isaiah warns against it. The Assyrians move south; soon Ahaz is their vassal; the Temple treasures are handed over and worship of Assyrian deities, even in the Temple, is encouraged. In 705 Hezekiah, successor to Ahaz, decides to break off the alliance with Assyria and seek Egyptian support, though again in the teeth of opposition from Isaiah. He soon pays the price. In 701 Sennacherib, new king of Assyria, marches towards Judah until Hezekiah is left, as the Assyrian records describe it, "like a bird in a cage". He tries to save the city by paying an enormous tribute to the enemy. There is uncertainty as to what precisely happens next, but the Assyrian army withdraws and Judah escapes by the skin of her teeth. She will not do so for ever.

2 Amos
– roaring for justice

Amos is a country shepherd, coming from Tekoa, a village about ten miles south of Jerusalem. He's also "a dresser of sycamore trees" (7:14): he punctures the fruit to make it ripen more quickly. Perhaps he takes on this extra work to supplement his meagre wages. If so, it would explain his deep empathy with the poor of Israel.

Amos will declare, "I am no prophet" – his way of saying he is not a prophet as his enemies understand the term, he is not a professional. But he is in no doubt that he speaks in God's name. He would hardly have launched himself into his risky task, had it not been for the conviction that he did so at the order of "The Lord [who] roars from Sion" (1:2). He travels to the north to do his own roaring on the Lord's behalf. With countryside imagery, he argues that prophecy is as inevitable as a lion roaring because it has found its prey, or a young lion growling in its lair because it wants to protect what it has caught. When a lion roars, he asks rhetorically, who would not be afraid? And when "the Lord God has spoken; who can but prophesy?" (3:8).

His prophetic career begins in about 760 BC, when Israel is enjoying material prosperity. Boundaries have been extended, new buildings are rising, religion seems to be flourishing. But the pleasant façade hides a dreadful fact: many northerners live in dire poverty, poverty in large measure due to the treatment they receive at the hands of the rich. Amos calls upon them to repent, to rid themselves of greed, hypocritical worship, appalling treatment of the poor. If not, disaster awaits them: they'll be marched off into exile. It's not a welcome message, even less so coming from the lips of a southerner. Predictably, he is soon asked to leave: the priest at Bethel tells him he should return to Judah where he belongs; he can do his prophesying there and be paid for it. But opposition only strengthens Amos' resolve to see the job through.

The lion roars

Initially, Amos wins the attention of his hearers by cataloguing the punishments about to befall Israel's neighbours – several of them her traditional enemies. For "crimes against humanity" and crimes without number ("three transgressions and... four"), they are to be punished. News of the impending disasters doubtless met with approval from his hearers, but not for long. It was a softening-up process, readying them for the oracle against themselves. If the Lord is to punish the pagans, how much more his own people! Their crimes are the greater because of what God did for them at the Exodus.

Their misdeeds include ill-treatment of the poor, summed up in the poignant accusation that they are ready to sell "the needy for a pair of sandals"; sexual impropriety; selfishness which leads those who have taken a "garment" as a pledge to hold on to it, though the law says it should be returned at the end of the day as a protection against cold nights; and excessive drinking even in the Temple courts. Amos warns, in a countryman's picture language, that they will be crushed by the Lord as if by a cart overloaded with sheaves. Their warriors will flee in shame (1:1 – 2:16).

Witnesses summoned

Amos presents a series of judgement scenes, each beginning with "Hear this word…" Israel may be God's chosen people, but the end is near: what remains will be like the remnants of a sheep – "legs, or a piece of an ear" – salvaged by the shepherd from a lion's mouth. (This is the first appearance in the prophets of the notion of "the remnant", the minority who survive and are a token of God's fidelity.) The shrine at Bethel will be destroyed, as will the luxury homes of the wealthy – "the winter house as well as the summer house" – and the opulent ivory furnishings. The prosperity of Jeroboam II's long reign has blinded them to what lies in store. There are bitter words for the pampered womenfolk, whom he addresses, with peasant rudeness, as "you cows of Bashan" (Bashan cattle being famed as plump and well-fed beasts!). They "oppress the poor, [and] crush the needy", concerned only that their husbands should ply them with drinks. Judgement has been passed: wrongdoers will be dragged away to destruction (3:1 – 4:3).

There may be abundant sacrifices, but it's all a cover-up: people cynically remark, "Come to [the shrine at] Bethel – and transgress", as though shrine devotions justify evil behaviour in other areas of life. They have had warnings – a series of natural disasters, such as drought (described as "cleanness of teeth"!) and blight, even one when the Lord saved them from their fate "like a brand snatched from the fire" – but, alas, "you did not return to me, says the Lord". That sad refrain leads up to the frightening words: "prepare to meet your God" (4:4-13).

Even now the people are urged to "seek me and live" rather than seeking help at their shrines. The northerners, who "trample on the poor", may have built themselves fine stone houses; they will never live in them. They may have planted pleasant vineyards; they will never drink their wine. They have made a mockery of justice by taking bribes and pushing aside "the needy" who seek redress. If only they would learn to "hate evil and love good", then "the God of hosts" might still "be gracious" to them. Amos insists that disaster will come and even the vineyards will join in the communal weeping (5:1-17).

"The day of the Lord"

Many in Israel look forward to "the day of the Lord", when, they believe, God will triumph and the chosen people rejoice. But Amos warns: "Alas for you who desire the day of the Lord!"; it will be a day of darkness, not of light; of judgement, not of festival. Any attempt to flee will be like fleeing from a lion only to meet with a bear, or resting your hand in apparent safety against a wall only to be bitten by a snake. As God's spokesman, he declares, "I despise your festivals"; they are so much hypocrisy. Instead, "let justice roll down like waters, and righteousness like an everflowing stream". "Alas" for those who lie back complacently and feel secure, sprawling on their "beds of ivory", singing "idle songs" to the strumming of the harp, drinking wine by the bowlful and anointing themselves with oil. In God's name, Amos warns: "I am raising up against you a nation." Who can doubt that the oppressor will be Assyria? (5:18 – 6:14).

Visions of disaster

In everyday things – locusts, a drought, a plumb line, a basket of ripe fruit – Amos reads a message from the Lord. A plague of locusts devouring "the latter growth" (the first crop was requisitioned by the king), and "a shower of fire" (a drought) are obvious threats to the people, and Amos pleads with the Lord, "How can Jacob [i.e. Israel] stand?" and adds movingly, "He is so small!" However, there is no relenting in the case of the next two visions, presumably because the people have failed to repent. The Lord's plumb line measures his people and shows them to be so warped as to be beyond correction. Similarly, the sight of a basket of ripe fruit tells Amos that the people are ripe for punishment

Between the third and fourth visions comes the attempt to get rid of Amos. Incensed by his preaching, the priest at the Bethel sanctuary reports to the king that Amos is saying the king will die by the sword and "Israel must go into exile". He says what is, sadly, all too true, "the land is not able to hear all his words". Amos is told to go home, but shows his mettle by going in his own time. He reminds the priest that it was the Lord who told him, "Go prophesy to my people", warns the priest of the fate awaiting him and reiterates that Israel will go into exile. Again he attacks those who "trample on the needy, and bring to ruin the poor of the land"; who cannot wait for the end of holy days (which put a temporary stop to business) so that they can get on with their trading; who falsify weights and measures; who are ready to sell the poor into slavery because of a trifling debt. God will see that feast days become days of grief, that mourning signs – sackclothed loins and shaven heads – appear; and there will be "a famine on the land; not a famine of bread… but of hearing the words of the Lord". They may wander from sea to sea in their seeking, but they will not find.

Amos sees the Lord "beside the altar" (perhaps at the Bethel shrine), striking the capitals so that the building collapses upon the people. They may dig down to the underworld or climb up to the heavens, may seek refuge in the heights of Mount Carmel or in the depths of the sea, but it will be in vain. Then come dreadful words for the northerners to hear: in God's sight, far-away nations, like the Ethiopians, are as important as the people of Israel. There are no exemptions for those who call themselves his people; if they sin they will perish (7:1 – 9:10).

Promise of restoration

The book ends with a conclusion as wonderful as it is unexpected – and perhaps added later (9:11-15). Despite the fact that God can never be blind to evil and that human wickedness has terrible consequences, God's mercy will prevail: David's dynasty will be restored – a promise finally fulfilled in the person of Jesus Christ. At the Council of Jerusalem (Acts 15:15-17) James quotes this passage and declares that, through the missionary work of Paul, David's dynasty will extend to the whole world, not by military might but by the humble confession that Jesus Christ is Lord.

Today's world is not so different from that which Amos knew: immense wealth and abundant food resources are found alongside extremes of hunger and poverty; the cry for justice for the poor is still raised; the danger of divorcing religious practice from daily living is as real as ever; and politicians sometimes behave as though their activities are exempt from the overriding demands of God's justice. The book of Amos is a tract for our times. The courageous shepherd-prophet did not roar in vain.

3 Hosea
– overwhelmed by divine love

Hosea's story is the story of a man who suffers the breakdown of his marriage, a tragedy profoundly influencing him and his message. Though not the first Hebrew to forgive an erring wife, he is the first to gain from that experience new insight into the steadfast love of the Lord for his wayward people; he likens the covenant to a marriage union, an idea never before found in the Bible, and is appalled that the people should have embraced Canaanite religious practices.

By delivering them from Egypt and leading them through the desert, the Lord had proved himself a Shepherd God, even a Warrior God, but could he also be an agricultural God, ensuring fruitfulness of crops and cattle? The Canaanites claimed they had just such a "god", Baal, and his consort Astarte. In the Canaanite fertility rites sacred prostitution was thought to ensure success of the crops. Hosea was horrified that such rites had been introduced into Hebrew shrines. Not only did they demean sexuality, they amounted to rejection of the Lord himself.

Like his contemporary Amos, Hosea prophesied in Israel, though, unlike Amos, he was a northerner, so that, while enjoying the advantage of working on home territory, he had the sadness of witnessing the death throes of his native land. His ministry began shortly after Amos' began (c.750 BC) and seems to have lasted through the chaotic days leading to the fall of the northern kingdom in 721, a time not only of political instability but also of the ever-growing Assyrian menace. If the Canaanite religious cult was one of the chief objects of Hosea's anger, the other was Israel's involvement in power games, their trusting in the big battalions rather than in God.

The marriage

It's not clear whether Hosea, son of Beeri, knew from the start that his wife Gomer had been involved in Canaanite fertility cults or whether it was only later that she proved unfaithful; in any event three children were born and at the Lord's direction given names at once unusual and richly significant. The eldest boy was called Jezreel, after the fertile valley running from Mount Carmel to above the Sea of Galilee, an area which witnessed an appalling massacre a century earlier: the boy would be living proof that God had not forgotten that dreadful deed. The significance of the names of their daughter and their second son – Lo-ruhamah, meaning "Unpitied", and Lo-ammi, meaning "Not my people" – was clear enough: Israel has forfeited its privileged position: "you are not my people and I am not your God" (1:1-11).

In his own agonising experience Hosea sees a reflection of the Lord's anguish. To those who worship Baal and his consort, the Lord makes an incredible announcement: he also has a wife – Israel! Alas, she has gone after "her lovers" (the Baals), saying, "they give me" all I need. But she is wrong: "it was I [the Lord] who gave" all; and now "I will take back" the good things she received from me (2:1-13).

Despite his wife's infidelities, Hosea is unable to reject her; he longs for a return to the days of courtship and early marriage, just as God says to Israel: "I will now allure her, and bring her back into the wilderness [the desert days were the ideal era of the relationship between the Lord and his people] and speak tenderly to her... There she shall respond as in the days of her youth" (2:14-15). The reconciliation, a new covenant, will have a transforming effect on the whole of nature: everywhere there will be peace.

Loving faithfulness and knowledge of God

Three times the Lord renews his betrothal commitment: "I will take you for my wife for ever" – in righteousness, justice, love, mercy and faithfulness; "and you shall know the Lord". Two phrases shine out like nuggets of gold. The first, "steadfast love" (*chesed*), which meant the virtues underlying a covenant – love, fidelity, loyalty – but with Hosea means the conditions demanded of an intimate personal relationship. This is borne out by the other striking expression: "you shall know the Lord". In the Bible "knowledge" (*da'ath*) is frequently used of the sexual relationship between husband and wife. "Only one thing constituted Israel... knowing the God that first knew them... On God's side it includes election, love, covenant, protection, and security; on Israel's side it is all that is involved in being a faithful, obedient, worshipping, holy people."[1] With this relationship re-established, everything will change: God will call upon the heavens to give the earth the sun and rain it needs, and the earth will produce its crops. With its literal meaning (that is, "God sows") in mind, Hosea refers to the new situation as "Jezreel". His children's names will be reversed: Israel will again receive pity and the covenant assurance, "You are my people", to which she will reply, "You are my God" (2:14-23).

---

[1] H.D. Beeby, *Grace Abounding: A Commentary on the Book of Hosea* (Grand Rapids, MI: Eerdmans, 1989), p. 140.

Hosea retells the story of his marriage in autobiographical form, showing that the motive for reconciliation with his wife is God's steadfast love; he will love her "as the Lord loves the people of Israel" despite their infidelities. Hosea pays a ransom to get her back, but for a while, until she proves her fidelity, they will not live as husband and wife. Similarly the Lord will subject his adulterous spouse to a period of testing, until she comes to her senses and returns "to the Lord and to his goodness" (3:1-5).

Indictment of Israel

Hosea presents the charge sheet against Israel, though occasionally offering glimmers of hope. *Chesed* makes demands on both covenant partners, but the Israelites have shown "no faithfulness or loyalty". There is "no knowledge [in the intimate sense explained above] in the land". All the commandments have been ignored; such conduct will have an adverse effect on the whole of nature.

The priests have failed to teach God's law. Worse still, they have exchanged "their glory", true worship of the Lord, for the "shame" of Baal rituals. Such behaviour will not benefit them in the slightest, and, inevitably, the people follow them so that "it shall be like people, like priest". They gather on mountaintops and in shady green groves, typical sites of pagan shrines, and there consult the local Baal, whom Hosea contemptuously describes as nothing more than "a piece of wood" with attendant furnishings. The people have become involved in "a spirit of whoredom", a reference not only to the licentious behaviour accompanying Baal worship but still more to the idolatry involved: since the Lord is in a marital relationship with his people, idolatry is tantamount to adultery. The shrines at Gilgal and Bethel (meaning "house of God" but scornfully renamed as Beth-aven, "house of emptiness") must be shunned because of their associations with the Baal cult. It's as though a "wind" of lustful desire has taken hold of them; they drink to excess and then besport themselves "in sexual orgies" (4:1-12).

Those who ought to have set an example have in fact led others astray; even in renowned sanctuaries, they have been "a snare" and "a net" to entangle the people. Israel may "go to seek the Lord, but they will not find him" and the children born as a result of involvement in the Baal cult are "illegitimate children" rather than blessings from the Lord (4:13 – 5:7).

Political instability and upheaval

Between the long, prosperous years of Jeroboam II and the brief reign of the last of the northern kings there was a span of only fourteen years; but it "produced seven kings, five dynasties, a major war from 736 to 732 and the loss of the northeast section of the kingdom to Assyria".[2] The people should have amended their ways and returned to God, but they have not done so. Hosea, speaking in God's name, warns them: "I will be like a lion to Ephraim… until they acknowledge their guilt and seek my face." Then, as though in response, the people cry: "Come, let us return to the Lord; for it is he who has torn us, and he will heal us… on the third day he will raise us up… let us press on to know the Lord." (The promise of national restoration "on the third day" brings to mind the Easter message of Jesus' resurrection "on the third day".) But this is only a transitory repentance; putting into words what he believes is going on in God's own heart, a tussle between the longing to save and the demands of justice, Hosea has the Lord declare: "What shall I do with you, O Ephraim? … Your love is like a morning cloud, like the dew that goes away early." What the Lord wants is "steadfast love (*chesed*) and not sacrifice, the knowledge (*da'ath*) of God rather than burnt offerings". Ritual activity is a sham unless underpinned by steadfast love and knowledge of God (5:8 – 6:6).

Unrepentant Israel will reap the whirlwind

Israel's crimes are enumerated: sacred shrines are scenes of wrongdoing; priests, behaving like brigands, prey upon worshippers. God admits that though "I would restore the fortunes of my people", they, including king and courtiers, have made that impossible through their wickedness. They are inflamed with passion and wine like "a heated oven". The people of Israel "devour their rulers". Hosea compares them, first, to a cake set to cook on a hot stone but not turned over, and so only half-baked; then, to a silly dove, fluttering from one nation to another – "they call upon Egypt, they go to Assyria" – in search of help, but never to the Lord; and finally to "a defective bow" which is useless to the archer. Again Hosea visualises the Lord expressing his anguish over his people's refusal to return to him: "I would redeem them," he says, "but they speak lies against me" (6:11 – 7:16).

Let "the trumpet" sound to warn of impending doom: "a vulture" hovers "over the house of the Lord". There is no point in crying to God, for "they have broken my covenant", setting up kings and princes, without divine approval, and making "idols", like the notorious "calf" that became their god. Then comes the terrifying warning: "they sow the wind, and they shall reap the whirlwind": crops will not flourish and even if they did, other nations would devour them. It's not to the Lord but to other nations they have turned, even to Assyria, looking for support. And so their days are

[2] C. Stuhlmueller CP, *Amos, Hosea, Micah, Nahum, Zephaniah, Habakkuk: Collegeville Bible Commentary*, no. 15 (Collegeville, MN: Liturgical Press, 1986), p. 45.

numbered; another exile awaits them, a "return to Egypt" from which the Lord originally rescued them (8:1-14).

They "have played the whore" and will pay for it with the sorrows of exile: they "shall not remain in the land of the Lord" nor will they have anywhere to worship "on the day of the festival of the Lord". They may denounce Hosea as "a fool", but that is an indication of their wickedness; he is "a sentinel" meant to warn of approaching danger, but has met only with opposition. They have sunk to the depths reached at Gibeah, a few miles from Jerusalem (once the scene of an outrage and an even more horrifying revenge [Judges 19 – 21]). The Lord rescued their ancestors when they were as vulnerable as "grapes in the wilderness"; but no sooner had they reached the threshold of the Promised Land than they got involved in the cult of Baal "and became detestable like the thing they loved". They will pay for it: "Ephraim's glory shall fly away like a bird"; its children will be short-lived, its women infertile. "I will love them no more" (9:1-15).

When Israel flourished, the people increased the number of pagan shrines and embellished the stone pillars, representing Baal. Even if they had a king, what could he do when Israel is unfaithful to the Lord? Instead of rejoicing in the Lord, they will be ashamed of their idol: it will be carried off to Assyria as war booty. The once famous shrine of Bethel, here referred to as "Aven" (Shame), will be destroyed and the people punished. Hosea urges repentance: "Sow for yourselves righteousness; reap steadfast love (*chesed*)… for it is time to seek the Lord, that he may come"; it is the Lord and not Baal who guarantees fruitfulness for their crops (10:1-12).

God's abiding love

Chapter 11, a high point of Old Testament revelation, depicts a God whose love is greater than the unfaithfulness of his creatures. If earlier the Lord appeared as husband, betrayed by his wife's unfaithfulness, here he appears as doting parent, wounded by a child's ingratitude. "When Israel was a child, I loved him" – like any parent, the Lord loved his children before they were able to make any response. It began at the Exodus when, taking the initiative, "out of Egypt I called my son". He describes the relationship in terms of what parents, especially mothers, do for their children: "I… taught Ephraim to walk", "took them up in my arms", "led them with cords of human kindness, with bands of love", "like those who lift infants to their cheeks, I bent down to them and fed them". Despite such love, "they kept sacrificing to the Baals, and offering incense to idols" (11:1-4).

If the Lord now punishes them, it will be like a parent reluctantly correcting a wayward child. With deep emotion, he cries out: "How can I give you up, Ephraim? How can I hand you over, O Israel? How can I treat you like Admah… [and] Zeboiim [notoriously wicked towns]? My heart recoils within me; my compassion grows warm and tender… I am God and no mortal, the Holy One in your midst" (11:8-9). In these verses "we penetrate deeper into the mind and heart of God than anywhere else in the Old Testament".[3]

Death sentence on Israel

After that merciful interlude, Hosea returns to his accusations. In a rather confused section, there is reference not only to current offences, such as making a treaty with Assyria and currying favour with Egypt, instead of relying on the Lord; but also to offences of their ancestors, such as the trickery of Jacob, which are attributed to them.

But there is no shortage of actual offences committed by Israel. And they are warned: "I will make you live in tents again", referring to the desert days, when they were conscious of God's closeness to them – but this time it will be the desert of exile. The Lord showed his loving concern by speaking through the prophets, but Israel's response has been a turning to the despicable rites of Baal. They have resorted to magic and have ended up doing reverence to idols, contemptuously spoken of: "People are kissing calves!" Their fate is sealed: they will last no longer than "morning mist" or "chaff that swirls from the threshing floor" or a column of "smoke" curling into the sky. Though the Lord has never ceased to care for them, they have forgotten him and so their Saviour will become their Judge. Judgement has been passed and is now "kept in store", as though on a scroll, awaiting implementation. A final terrible sentence reminds them of the fate often awaiting a conquered nation – "little ones… dashed in pieces", "pregnant women ripped open" (11:12 – 13:16).

Repentance and salvation

However, the book of Hosea ends on a note of optimism. The prophet has already hinted that the people must not lose faith in God. Now he bids them "return to the Lord": they must promise not to look to Assyria for help nor ever again to address their idols, "the work of [their] hands" as "Our God". Then the Lord will be generous: he will "heal their disloyalty", "love them freely", be "like the dew" (producing fruitfulness even in the long dry season). Israel will be transformed in beauty and fruitfulness; but all this

---

3 Beeby, *Grace Abounding*, p. 140.

comes not from the Baals but from the Lord, the God who loves them with the steadfast love of a husband who cannot reject an unfaithful wife or of a parent who cannot bear to put aside his ungrateful children (14:1-9).

In the words of a modern scholar: "Theologically, the book of Hosea is the most important of the Twelve (minor) Prophets... It stands with... Isaiah and Jeremiah at the pinnacle of prophetic thought."[4] It is a wonderful preparation for the coming of him who will be the fullest revelation of God's overwhelming love and compassion.

---

[4] James M. Ward, *Thus Says the Lord* (Nashville: Abingdon Press, 1991), p. 215.

4 Isaiah I
– dazzled by holiness

Isaiah, son of Amoz, was born in about 765 BC. Some twenty years later began a prophetic career that would span almost half a century and the reigns of four of Judah's kings. He was married – his wife was a prophetess (8:3) – and had two sons, who, like Hosea's children, bore strange but significant names. He was a man of influence, with ready access to the king. Unlike Amos and Hosea, his mission was directed to the southern kingdom: Jerusalem was his city; he loved it dearly and yet was compelled to reproach it.

This was a turbulent time, with Assyria a serious threat to both Israel and Judah; shortly after the accession of Tiglath-Pileser III in 745 aggressive Assyrian campaigns began and by the end of the century the southern kingdom alone survived. Several times Isaiah saw Assyrian forces at the gates and viewed them as instruments of punishment for an unfaithful city. He urged Judah's kings to act with confidence in the Lord but met with little success. He inspired disciples, imbued with his concerns and eager to apply them to the circumstances of their own day. This "Isaian school" carried on his work for several centuries. Thus, of the sixty-six chapters that make up the book of Isaiah, only chapters 1–39 are attributable to Isaiah of eighth-century Jerusalem. Chapters 40–55 (Isaiah II) reflect the situation of the exile in the sixth century and chapters 56–66 (Isaiah III) the situation after the exile when the Jewish community tried to rebuild itself; both sections re-echo major themes of Isaiah I – God's holiness, transcendence and Lordship of history; and Jerusalem's importance as humankind's unique hope for the future.

The call

The story of Isaiah's call in chapter 6 explains not only how his prophetic ministry began but also what inspired his mission. In the year of Uzziah's death (742), he is standing in prayer at the threshold of the Holy of Holies, when suddenly its dark interior is ablaze with light, and there is "the Lord sitting on a throne, high and lofty", towering above the Temple so that only "the hem of his robe" fills the sanctuary. Attendant angels, six-winged "seraphs", reverently cover their faces and cry out, "Holy, holy, holy". The Hebrew word for holiness (*qadosh*) denotes separateness, otherness. God is thrice holy, totally Other, utterly Transcendent: "the whole earth is full of his glory". The door posts shudder and the Temple is "filled with smoke" which, like the cloud above Sinai (Exodus 19:16-25), is a sign of God's presence.

Isaiah is acutely aware of his unworthiness and that of his people. A seraph applies a burning, purifying coal to his lips so that he is able to respond: "Here am I; send me!" His prophetic ministry is launched, and the memory of God's blinding holiness will colour his preaching and give him strength to face every difficulty; his people may "stop their ears, and shut their eyes", yet he sees a glimmer of hope: the nation may be like a tree destined to be cut down, but its destruction will not be total – a "stump" will remain.

Indictment of Judah

Like Amos and Hosea, Isaiah condemns greed, hypocrisy, lack of trust in God and the making of appeals to foreign nations for help. In 721 the northern kingdom fell and he is convinced the same fate awaits Judah if it does not repent; its people "have despised the Holy One of Israel" with a sinfulness comparable to that of Sodom and Gomorrah. In apparent reference to the devastation caused by Sennacherib's invasion in 701, the land is compared to a person who has been waylaid and in whom "from the sole of the foot even to the head, there is no soundness"; only the Lord saved "daughter Zion" from total ruin (1:4-9).

But now he warns that "though you make many prayers, I will not listen" because they have no care for "the oppressed… the orphan… [or] the widow". Yet even now, if they repent, "though [their] sins are like scarlet, they shall be like snow". Jerusalem, "the faithful city", has become the unfaithful city, "a whore". The Lord will punish her, but the punishment will be purifying and she will again be styled faithful, and will be the Lord's agent for the salvation of all peoples, so that "the mountain of the Lord's house" (where Isaiah met the God of holiness) will stand in moral stature as "the highest of the mountains" and "all the nations shall stream to it". Warfare will end and world peace be established, so that "they shall beat their swords into ploughshares, and their spears into pruning hooks; nation shall not lift up sword against nation, neither shall they learn war any more".[1] But a vision of future glory cannot pardon present sinfulness: many are involved in idolatry ("their land is filled with idols"), or seek security in riches (the "land is filled with silver and gold") and in armaments ("there is no end to their chariots"). If only they would "walk in the light of the Lord" (1:10 – 2:8)!

---

[1] These words are enshrined opposite the United Nations HQ, New York.

"That day"

Like Amos, Isaiah warns that "the day of the Lord" will be a day of darkness (2:5 – 4:6): "On that day", amid the near-anarchy in Jerusalem, boys will become princes; and leaders, taking over the homes of ordinary people, will grind the faces of the poor. "On that day" the women will suffer; they are haughty, "mincing along as they go"; their fripperies (Isaiah gives an impressive inventory of their apparel) symbolise the luxury of the nation; they will have their "well-set hair" shorn and be carried off to exile in sackcloth. So many men will fall in battle that "seven women shall take hold of one man", happily making provision for themselves so long as they can be spared the "disgrace" of being without a husband. "On that day" the faithless will indeed be punished but a "branch", like the remnant in Amos, will escape and blossom and "whoever is left in Zion… will be called holy", like their holy God. As the Lord guided his people by pillars of cloud and fire, so now he "will create over the whole site of Mount Zion… a cloud by day and smoke and the shining of a flaming fire by night".

The Song of the Vineyard (chapter 5) sums up the situation. The vineyard is Israel and its owner, the Lord, has spared no effort to make it fruitful. What more could I have done, he asks, "that I have not done"? But it has produced only "wild grapes". In a series of six woes (5:8-30) Isaiah condemns those who increase their estates at the expense of the poor; who indulge in strong drink from morning to night; who seem to pull at evil as though with "cart ropes" and who, imagining the day of the Lord will be glorious, beg that "the plan of the Holy One of Israel [may] hasten to fulfilment"; those who "call evil good and good evil"; who are wise in their own eyes; and who "acquit the guilty for a bribe, and deprive the innocent of their rights". All "have despised the word of the Holy One"; "the anger of the Lord" has been aroused; he will act through "a nation far away": he has only to whistle and the Assyrians will come "swiftly, speedily", like a young lion about to seize and carry off its prey.

"Long live the king"

If God's holiness is a major theme of Isaiah, chapters 7–11 show that another is the city of Jerusalem and in particular its king, who, according to biblical tradition (cf. 2 Samuel 7), is a son of God whose dynasty will last for ever.

The second year of King Ahaz's reign (734) brought a crisis: Syria and Ephraim (the northern kingdom) tried to bar an Assyrian advance and, when Judah refused to join them, laid siege to Jerusalem and "the heart of [the] people shook as the trees of the forest shake before the wind". Accompanied by his son, Isaiah went to meet Ahaz. The lad's name, Shear-jashub ("a remnant shall return"), symbolises that even if Judah is destroyed, a remnant will return. The prophet bids Ahaz not to fear: the enemy leaders are as harmless as "smouldering stumps", and if he will only stand firm, all will be well. (Ignoring the advice, Ahaz sought Assyrian help, and Judah became an Assyrian vassal, saddled with a heavy annual tribute.)

Isaiah invites the king to ask for "a sign of the Lord" to authenticate his message. When he declines, Isaiah assures him that he will get a sign all the same: a young woman (*almah*) "shall bear a son, and shall name him Immanuel" ("God-with-us"). He will be fed on "curds and honey" and before he knows "to refuse the evil and choose the good" the kings besieging Judah will no longer pose a threat. The "young woman" of his prophecy is probably Ahaz's wife.[2] Her child, Hezekiah, will in due course be king but, unlike his father, a worthy representative of the Davidic dynasty and a sign of the Lord's abiding presence with his people. His food will be a meagre diet of "curds and honey" because times are hard, but soon the lands of the enemies that now threaten will be deserted. But, warns Isaiah, then the real enemy will appear – Assyria. As if to underline the warning, he takes "a large tablet" and writes upon it, in letters big enough for all to see, the name of his second son: Maher-shalal-hash-baz ("quick spoil, speedy plunder"), another pointer to the threatening Assyrian invasion. Before his son is able to cry "My father" or "My mother", Damascus (capital of Syria) and Samaria (capital of the northern kingdom) will already have fallen to Assyria. Isaiah promises that since the people have rejected the gentle "waters of Shiloah" – that is, Jerusalem, dwelling place of the holy God – by turning for help to Assyria, Assyria's mighty river "will sweep on into Judah as a flood". But nations, however mighty, are nothing before the Lord and Isaiah must remember "God is with us" and refuse to share in the fears of his fellow citizens (7:1 – 8:22).

Isaiah again speaks of a king, but the emphasis is on the royal duties, especially that of establishing justice and peace. Those parts of the northern kingdom first to be overrun and made into Assyrian provinces – Zebulun and Naphtali – will be restored, so that the "people who walked in darkness" will see light and will rejoice as at harvest time. (Matthew 4:13-16 sees these words fulfilled when Jesus appears, not in the holy city but in the half-pagan region of Galilee.) The paraphernalia of war – "rod of their oppressor", boots of trampling warriors, "garments rolled in blood" – will be destroyed

---

[2] In reference to Jesus' birth, Matthew sees a new depth of meaning in Isaiah 7:10-17: if Ahaz's successor was a source of hope, the birth of the Messiah will bring hope to the whole world; again, the Hebrew word *almah* (young woman of marriageable age) is translated in the Greek version used by Matthew specifically as "virgin" and so admirably suits the evangelist's presentation of the virginal conception; and finally "Emmanuel" ("God with us") expresses Jesus' abiding presence. See R. Brown, *The Birth of the Messiah* (London: G. Chapman, 1977), pp. 143f.

because "a child has been born for us, a son given to us". The reference is to the coronation of a king, which was regarded as the king's rebirth as son of God. Astounding names are given him – "Wonderful Counsellor, Mighty God, Everlasting Father, Prince of Peace". No king of Israel ever fulfilled the job description implied by these lofty titles (9:1-7).

Isaiah threatens Assyria with punishment, for though the Lord used this "rod" for the punishment of his people, it has acted with excessive cruelty, arrogantly claiming that the enterprise was its own achievement and as effortless as collecting eggs from a bird's nest when "none… moved a wing… or chirped". Though Judah will suffer, a "remnant" will survive, made up of those who "lean on the Lord, the Holy One of Israel" – a fulfilment of the prophetic name of Isaiah's son. The Assyrian army may draw closer but will never do anything more than "shake [its] fist" at the holy city, and in the end will be totally destroyed (9:8 – 10:34).

Once more Isaiah speaks of a king whose coming will mark a renewal of the Davidic dynasty: he will be a "shoot… from the stump of Jesse" (King David's father). Endowed with "the spirit of the Lord", he will possess an array of attributes – wisdom and understanding, counsel and knowledge; he will judge "with righteousness" and not by appearances. It will be a returned paradise: all the animals will live together and will be so harmless that "a little child shall lead them"; and "the earth will be full of the knowledge of the Lord as the waters cover the sea". The benefits of the reign will spread to all the nations: the God of Israel is the God of the universe (11:1-10).

Fittingly, this section on the king finishes with a psalm-like song of thanksgiving for the time when Israel will enjoy final deliverance and God will be hailed as "my strength", "my might" and "my salvation". Those who are saved are urged to "shout aloud and sing for joy" because "great in your midst is the Holy One of Israel", the One whose holiness had dazzled Isaiah (11:11 – 12:6). The full implications of Isaiah's exalted picture of the future king were never remotely realised until a child was born who was truly Son of God, literally "Immanuel", God-with-us (see Matthew 1:23); to him was given the throne of David and his reign is to last for ever (Luke 1:32-33).

Nations, beware!

As in Amos, a series of "oracles against the nations" (chapters 13–23) features in Isaiah, though it ranges widely to include Babylon, the superpower that succeeded Assyria, and Egypt, a powerful nation whose assistance Judah often sought. It was to counter this tendency to seek Egyptian help that Isaiah paraded himself "naked and barefoot" (20:2), dramatising the humiliation that would befall Egyptian prisoners of war. There is even a promise of Egypt's conversion to the God of Israel and, in a final fantasy, Israel ranking along with Egypt and Assyria as one of the big three world powers (19:16-25)! There are several striking features about these oracles, some of which may date from after Isaiah.

First, they show that the power of the God of Israel is universal. Second, they condemn arrogance and idolatry. Third, unrelieved threats of doom are counterbalanced in the case of Judah by promises of restoration. Finally, they exhibit a vindictiveness and desire for revenge which, however unacceptable, are perhaps understandable among subject people, forever struggling for freedom. The judgement against Jerusalem includes the threat of destruction, perhaps that of 701 which involved the devastation of almost fifty Judaean cities and caused the prophet to "weep bitter tears… for the destruction of my beloved people" (22:4). It led the Judaeans to panic but not to trust in God; and when the threat passed, they turned to feasting – "Let us eat and drink, for tomorrow we die" (22:13) – rather than repentance.

"Last things"

Chapters 24–27 are often referred to as "the apocalypse of Isaiah". Apocalypse (literally, revelation) is a type of literature that draws back the veil to reveal the working out of God's plans, especially those concerned with the "last things"; it often speaks of universal judgement, a final banquet and salvation. Such themes, intermingled with other types of literature, promise that ultimately suffering and destruction will fall into perspective. Chapter 24 speaks of a world made desolate, referring perhaps to a particular incident, such as a drought, but standing as a more general warning of what happens when people "have transgressed laws, violated the statutes, broken the everlasting covenant". Everyone suffers – a city becomes a "city of chaos"; there is no distinction between different classes: "as with the slave, so with his master"; "the earth [is]… utterly laid waste"; "the wine dries up" and so "the noise of the jubilant" ceases. On the "day of the Lord" the repercussions of his wrath will be felt in heaven as well as on earth. But these disasters have an unexpected consequence: "From the ends of the earth we hear songs of praise… to the Righteous One" and finally "the Lord of hosts will reign on Mount Zion".

Chapter 25 describes the wonderful final banquet prepared by the Lord "on this mountain" (Zion), a banquet of delicious "rich food" and "well-aged wines". It will be "for all peoples" and the Lord "will swallow up death for ever", "wipe away the tears from all faces" and remove the reproach of his people. There will be rejoicing "in his salvation" and those who opposed his people will be punished. The theme of a final messianic banquet became current in Judaism and appears in the New Testament: Matthew 22:2-10; Luke 14:16-24 and Apocalypse 19:1-10.

A beautiful psalm of trust praises the Lord's final vindication of his people, when Jerusalem will be "a strong city", its gates wide open for the entry of "the righteous". "Your name", cries the poet, "and your renown are the soul's desire," and he adds a personal prayer: "My soul yearns for you… my spirit within me earnestly seeks you." By contrast, the wicked "do not see the majesty of the Lord"; though they once "ruled over us", they are now dead. For long enough God's people have writhed like a woman in travail, unable to bring forth; now, however, there is to be a rebirth of the nation. They are invited to take shelter while the Lord completes his destruction of their enemies, including the slaying of "Leviathan" (also called the dragon or the serpent), a mythical monster representing all that is evil (26:1 – 27:1).

A series of oracles speak of "that day" – a future time when the Lord will speak lovingly of his people as his fruitful vineyard. He himself will "guard it night and day", so that it will no longer fail to please him. Israel will crush the stones of the altars and the accoutrements of worship found outside Jerusalem, and at the sound of "a great trumpet" the scattered children of Israel "will come and worship the Lord on the holy mountain in Jerusalem" (27:2-13).

Trust in the Lord, not in Egypt

Eight chapters (28–35) offer alternating threats of judgement and promises of salvation. They seem to date largely from the end of the eighth century when, against Isaiah's advice, Hezekiah, King of Judah, rebelled against Assyria and sought Egypt's aid. By that alliance the southern kingdom "made a covenant with death". A bed "too short to stretch" out in, and a "covering too narrow" to wrap around its occupant are lively images for those who find no rest because they ignore the Lord. "Ariel" (Jerusalem) is warned that it will be besieged though threats suddenly give way to promise of salvation, with the enemy vanishing like "a vision of the night". Those who take up arms against the holy city are like a hungry or thirsty person who dreams of food or drink but wakes up unsatisfied! However, there is still a charge laid against Jerusalem's leaders: they behave with as little sense as people who are drunk. Their empty worship – their "hearts are far from me" – and their secret negotiations with Egypt indicate lack of trust in God. In fact "Egypt's help is worthless and empty"; she is "Rahab" (the name for a mythical sea monster), already subdued by the Lord (28:1 – 30:7).

A record is to be kept of people who welcome a false prophet who speaks "smooth things" but reject one prophesying "what is right". The former dares to say: "let us hear no more about the Holy One of Israel", but the Holy One warns that like a bulging wall or a potter's jar they are about to crash down in smithereens. Isaiah's advice for them and their king is: return to the Lord and rest in him – "in quietness and in trust shall be your strength". The Lord "waits to be gracious to you"; once they give up their idols, he will give them rain and heal their wounds and they will rejoice as on a day of festival. It is folly to seek an alliance with Egypt, "but… not look to the Holy One of Israel". Assyria will fall in the end and there will be "a king [who] will reign in righteousness" – unlike the messianic prophecies of chapters 9–11, there is no suggestion here that he will be of the Davidic line – and justice will spread through the land and "a villain" will no longer be honoured. Complacent women of the countryside are warned of an impending (though unspecified) disaster; but in the end tragedy will give way to bliss: when "a spirit from on high is poured out" the people will know "justice" and "righteousness" and "peace" (30:8 – 32:20).

After a brief threat against the enemy (Assyria or Babylon), chapter 33 continues with a prayer that the Lord, who "dwells on high", may "be gracious" to his people and an acknowledgement that "fear of the Lord is Zion's treasure". A brief description of the unhappy situation in the land leads the Lord to respond: "Now I will arise"; and his presence will cause fear among "the sinners in Zion". "Who among us", they cry, "can live with the devouring fire?" And back comes the answer: only those who "walk righteously" – who avoid oppression, bribes, hearing or seeing what is evil – only they "will live on the heights", their supply of food and water secure. The chapter ends with the invitation to admire the restored Jerusalem of the future, with the Lord "in majesty" dwelling in its midst and a river system bringing prosperity to the land.

The final two chapters (34–35) form a diptych of God's judgement: on one hand, the nations are summoned, Edom in particular, to hear judgement described in gory detail – upon all who have warred against Israel; on the other, Israel is depicted in its glory, with a highway stretching across the desert to bring back the exiles; the desert itself will "rejoice and blossom" and for "the thirsty ground" there will be springs of water.

Sennacherib's invasion

The final chapters are an appendix, taken almost word for word from 2 Kings 18:13 – 20:19. Chapters 36 and 37 deal with the Assyrian invasion, launched by King Sennacherib in 701, and poetically recorded in Lord Byron's "The

Destruction of Sennacherib": "The Assyrian came down like the wolf on the fold…" The invasion was brought to an end because either Sennacherib was forced to withdraw when he received news that the Egyptians were moving against him, or, as Isaiah 37:9-36 suggests, the Assyrian army was destroyed by a divine intervention.

Chapters 38–39 report King Hezekiah's remarkable recovery from sickness and the embassy sent by Babylon on hearing of the king's restoration to health: Hezekiah proudly parades his wealth before them, but Isaiah warns him that a time will come when the Babylonians will relieve him of all his possessions and reduce some of his subjects to slavery. The prophet's words are a bridge to Isaiah II, which unfolds against the backcloth of Babylonian exile.

The book of Isaiah includes some of the most magnificent poetry and prose in the Bible. With its hints of what is to come in passages about Immanuel and about the messianic king, it seems a natural companion to the New Testament, and in fact is quoted there more frequently than any other book of the Old Testament, with the possible exception of the Psalter.

5 Micah
– preaching true religion

Micah comes from the village of Moresheth in the Judaean foothills, twenty miles to the south-west of Jerusalem. He would have heard of the advances of the Assyrian army, may even have experienced some of its ravages, but makes no direct reference to them. Nor does he mention the Syro-Ephraimite conflict (735 BC) and the threat it posed to Jerusalem. But he does speak of Sennacherib's invasion in 701 (1:8-16): it has been suggested that that invasion caused him to flee and that it was as a refugee in Jerusalem that he gained first-hand knowledge of the city's corruption. He has left no record of his father's name, an indication perhaps of lowly social status; nor of how "the word of the Lord came to" him.

His mission, like Isaiah's, was particularly to Jerusalem and took place in about the last quarter of the eighth century. He has been unflatteringly described as "un Isaïe en sabots"[1] (an Isaiah in clogs). Isaiah is from the city, Micah from the countryside; Isaiah a person of prestige, Micah of humble origin; Isaiah a sophisticated writer, Micah less gifted, though able to wield powerful images and indulge in puns. Overshadowed by his illustrious contemporary, Micah still makes a distinctive contribution because his voice represents that of the ordinary village man or woman. He may witness the same events as Isaiah but sees them through different eyes, those of a peasant. He is a bitter opponent of hypocrisy, greed and injustice, a champion of the poor and an upholder of genuine worship. His many warnings of divine judgement on Jerusalem are relieved by promises of divine forgiveness. "Survivors" of the people will be gathered like sheep and return to the "fold" (2:12); a restored Jerusalem will be a key feature of God's universal rule.

Judah on trial

The Lord is coming in majesty "from his holy temple" to preside in judgement of his people. His awesome presence melts mountains "like wax near the fire". The world is summoned to "hear" the condemnation of the northern kingdom (called "Jacob" after its great ancestor), for idol worship and the accompanying rituals. It will be devastated. Micah notes that the sins of Jerusalem are the sins of Samaria, which has already suffered at the hands of Sennacherib. Many of the places levelled by his marauding army are mentioned by name, their fate often indicated by a play on words; for example, Beth-leaphrah means "city of dust", and the city of that name is made to "roll in the dust" (1:2-16)!

---

[1] P. Auvray, *La Bible et son Message* (May 1970), p. 6.

Micah focuses upon the social injustices perpetrated by land-grabbers who scheme on their beds how to take over the fields and homes of the poor and rise early to put their plans into operation. Well, God has plans for them. Their lands will be parcelled out among their enemies, and there will be nothing for them when the kingdom is restored for they no longer belong to "the assembly of the Lord". The Lord's words promise good to those who walk "uprightly", not to those who rob the poor of the garment that ought to be returned at sundown, turn women out of home and rob children of their inheritance. "Arise and go" into exile, he bids them, adding that the only prophets they will listen to are those who "preach to you of wine and strong drink".

Then it's the turn of the leaders, and the invective is harsher than ever. As in a lawsuit, they are commanded to "listen"; they who should know the meaning of justice "hate the good and love the evil", "tear the skin off my people", treating them as a butcher treats animals. They may cry to the Lord but "he will hide his face from them". As for the (false) prophets, they are utterly self-serving. They too will receive no answer from God. In striking contrast, Micah, a genuine prophet, "filled… with the spirit of the Lord", is not afraid to condemn the people's sins. "Hear this," he cries again, launching into a further attack upon the leaders. They "abhor justice", building "Zion with blood", giving "judgement for a bribe". The priests "teach for a price", the prophets "give oracles for money", and yet these leaders have the gall to say, "Surely the Lord is with us!" Because of their wrongdoing Zion will become like a ploughed field, its city like "a heap of ruins", its sacred mount like a wooded hill (2:1 – 3:12).

Promise of renewal

A vision opens up of what will happen in "days to come": instead of Jerusalem reduced to rubble, it is Jerusalem raised to a towering height and drawing to herself like a magnet all peoples and nations. The Lord will "teach [them] his ways"; and there will be universal peace, with peasants sitting peacefully under their vines and fig trees. Though other nations may come "each in the name of its god", "we", Micah proudly proclaims, "will walk in the name of the Lord our God for ever and ever". Like a shepherd the Lord gathers the lame, the outcasts and the afflicted, and leads this "remnant" into the sheepfold of Jerusalem, and "daughter Zion" will regain her former glory.

Judah is described as being in exile – a sign that this passage is a later addition. There is "no king", Jerusalem is like a woman in the pains of childbirth, and the people "go forth from the city" and "to Babylon". This grim prospect is softened by a promise that "the Lord will redeem you from the hands of your enemies". Many nations muster against Jerusalem and they may have their plans, but the Lord has his plans, too – to gather them like "sheaves" at harvest time; and "daughter Zion" is to join in the threshing.

After referring to the humiliation suffered by Hezekiah, whose foolish revolt against Assyria led to Sennacherib's invasion, Micah looks forward to a future Davidic king, coming from "Bethlehem". Though insignificant, its association with King David means that it is "from ancient days". "She who is in labour" will deliver a son who will shepherd his people and "be the one of peace". Should Assyria, the arch-enemy, attempt to enter the land, it will meet with defeat at the hands of Judah's chieftains. The Lord's people will be involved in the salvation of all nations, like the refreshing "dew from the Lord", but also in their punishment, for "the remnant of Jacob" will be "like a lion". Moreover, the Lord will cut away human supports, such as military might ("horses" and "chariots"), idol worship and recourse to divination, but promises by implication that his people will be supported by an era of peace and strong faith (4:1 – 5:14).

Renewed trial of Jerusalem

The repeated cry, "Hear", indicates that the Lord is again presiding over a lawsuit against his people, but this is judgement on a cosmic scale, with "hills", "mountains" and "foundations" acting as witnesses. Though the Lord will be both accuser and judge, he speaks with anguish, reminding "my people" of all he has done for them (bringing them "up from the land of Egypt" and leading them safely to the Promised Land) but also plaintively enquiring: "In what have I wearied you? Answer me!" (The question inspired the "reproaches" in Good Friday's liturgy.) The people ask what they must do: more liturgical worship, more burnt offerings, even "thousands of rams… ten thousands of rivers of oil"? Or, most terrible of all, are they to try and curry favour by offering their own children in sacrifice? The prophet reminds them that they have already been told what they are to do; he recalls the essence of true religion in memorable words: "This is what Yahweh asks of you: only this, to act justly, to love tenderly and to walk humbly with your God" (*Jerusalem Bible* translation).

The trial scene continues, with the Lord detailing some of "the treasures of wickedness" among his people: merchants who swindle, wealthy people who use violence against the poor, lies and deceit everywhere. With a list of punishments that reflects Micah's village background, the people are warned that they will experience hunger and poverty; they will sow but not reap; they will tread olive and grape but never anoint themselves with the oil or taste the wine. They have behaved like the people of the north who followed evil kings, and so Jerusalem will meet the same fate as Samaria. Micah laments his own situation: he finds no one who is "faithful"; everywhere there is bloodshed, "hands... skilled to do evil", officials who "ask for a bribe", powerful people who dictate what they want and "pervert justice"; a lack of trust even between husband and wife, and families divided. At the end of this devastating catalogue, he warns: "The day of... punishment has come." But then, in an act of amazing personal confidence, he declares: "as for me... I will wait for the God of my salvation" (6:1 – 7:7).

God's steadfast love

Confident of God's love, Jerusalem warns her enemies: "Do not rejoice over me," for, though I sit in darkness because of my sins, the Lord "will bring me out to the light" and those who mockingly ask, "Where is the Lord your God?" will be put to shame. On that "day" the city walls will be rebuilt, boundaries extended and exiles brought back from far-away lands; and their prayerful hope is that their shepherd-God will "let them feed in Bashan and Gilead" (symbols of fruitfulness and plenty), as he did at the Exodus "in the days of old". And the book of Micah is brought to its close with a hymn of praise for God, who is incomparable in "pardoning iniquity", "delights in showing clemency... [and] will show faithfulness" in accordance with the promises given to Abraham and "our ancestors from the days of old" (7:8-20).

Almost a hundred years after his death, Micah's words were being quoted to draw people to conversion (Jeremiah 26:18); and over two thousand years later his prophecy of a future ruler born in Bethlehem is dear to Christians everywhere, as are his words about what is demanded of all true followers of the Lord: "only this, to act justly, to love tenderly and to walk humbly with your God" (6:8).

The seventh-century prophets

The southern kingdom's escape from Sennacherib in 701 BC was a close-run thing. For the next half-century Judah is swamped by Assyrian influences and culture; its religious heritage is threatened; after the ministries of Isaiah and Micah no prophetic voice will be heard for fifty years. Judah might have been expected to learn from the disaster that befell the northern kingdom, but such was not the case. True, King Hezekiah (715–686) makes attempts at religious reform, but his son Manasseh (686–642) is the worst ruler Judah ever had: an Assyrian lackey, he pays a huge tribute and undoes his father's reforms by reinstating pagan altars in the Temple, introducing star worship and resorting to human sacrifice. 2 Kings 21:13 gives a picturesque description of how God will cleanse the city: "I will wipe Jerusalem as one wipes a dish, wiping it and turning it upside down" in the sink!

However, the latter half of the seventh century witnesses two events of huge import for God's people. First, the accession in 640 of King Josiah, grandson of the notorious Manasseh. With the might of Assyria on the wane, he is encouraged to restore Judah's former glory and embarks upon religious reforms that lead to the removal of pagan shrines and altars. In the eighteenth year of his reign, fresh impetus is given to reform by the discovery, in the course of Temple renovations, of the book we now know as Deuteronomy. It powerfully underlines the lesson taught by the great eighth-century prophets: Jerusalem's status as God's city will not save it from disaster; it must recognise the demands of justice, get rid of pagan practices and worship its one God in one place – the Temple. In the Temple "the Book of the Law" is read out to the people; they renew their covenant with the Lord and celebrate a Passover feast.

The reform would not have been possible but for the second key event, the collapse of Assyria. At the start of the century its power had never been greater, but during the next seventy-odd years it begins to unravel until in 612 its capital, Nineveh, falls to the Babylonians. The rejoicing in Judah is short-lived: Babylonia, under Nebuchadnezzar, proves as ambitious for conquests as the Assyrian power it replaces. During the siege of Nineveh, Egypt, the other dominant power in the Middle East, goes to the defence of the Assyrians, and Josiah, for an inexplicable reason, leads out his army to block the path of the Egyptians. He perishes in the attempt and "all Judah and Jerusalem mourned" for him (2 Chronicles 35:24). His son Jehoahaz reigns for only three months before the Egyptians, who now have Judah in their control, replace him with his half-brother Jehoiakim (609–598), though the latter is little more than a puppet-ruler. The people are largely pro-Egyptian in sympathy, but when in 605 at the battle of Carchemish Nebuchadnezzar, king of the Babylonians, defeats the Egyptians, Jehoiakim transfers his allegiance to Babylon, while continuing to look for an opportunity to regain independence. The moment arrives a few years later, when Babylonian forces, after attempting to invade Egypt, are forced to retreat; he then decides to withhold tribute from the Babylonians. That decision spells rebellion, and before long, though few realise it, Judah's own destruction.

The second half of the seventh century not only witnesses two crucial events – the reform of Josiah and the fall of Assyria – but also hears once more the voice of the prophets. Three are closely associated with the events just recalled: ZEPHANIAH, in the early days of Josiah's reign; NAHUM, a few years later; and HABAKKUK, just before the turn of the century. The seventh century also sees the appearance of JEREMIAH, a giant among prophets; but since his life and teaching are so closely linked with the fall of Jerusalem and the exile that follows, it is appropriate to deal with them in a later chapter.

Zephaniah, Nahum and Habakkuk
– rejoicing in Assyria's decline and fall

Zephaniah

"The word" came to Zephaniah, son of Cushi, "in the days of King Josiah" (640–609 BC). His fierce denunciation of idolatrous practices, rapacious judges and unjust merchants suggests that he prophesied before Josiah's reform. Like the eighth-century prophets, he begs the people to have no truck with pagan worship and warns that the worship of the Lord is incompatible with Baal worship and worship of the gods of other lands, such as the Ammonite god Milcom (1:1-6).

Like Amos and Isaiah, Zephaniah has a series of oracles against foreign nations (2:4-15). But his main concern is with Jerusalem, for "the day of the Lord" – an expression several times repeated – "is at hand", a day not of rejoicing and of light, but of moaning and of darkness. (This description of the day of the Lord inspired the doleful *Dies Irae* which used to be heard at every Requiem Mass and seems to be responsible for the grim picture that many have of the Last Day.) On that day wailing will be heard from various quarters of the city, for the Lord "will search Jerusalem with lamps" in pursuit of evildoers: it will be a day of dreadful consequences for all who defy the Lord. The only ones for whom there will be hope on that day are the "humble of the land" (in the Bible the "humble" [*anawim*] are specially dear to God. In Zephaniah the word assumes moral significance: it refers to those who submit themselves to God's will[1]) (1:7 – 2:3).

Jerusalem's officials behave like "roaring lions", looking for prey, her judges like "evening wolves" who leave nothing behind by the morning; her prophets are "faithless", her priests ignorant of the law. The city is warned to "wait for me"! But even now there is a promise that the people will "not be put to shame" because the Lord will purge them of the proud and arrogant and leave in their place a precious "remnant", "a people humble and lowly". The book comes to an end in a passage, possibly a later addition, in which Zion is urged to "rejoice and exult with all your heart": enemies have been defeated and the Lord is in the midst. He is pictured as renewing them "in his love" and exulting over them "with loud singing as on a day of festival" – or, as the *New Jerusalem Bible* translates it, dancing with shouts of joy over them (3:1-20).

---

[1] See *The New Jerusalem Bible*, ed. H. Wansbrough (London: Darton, Longman & Todd, 1985), p. 1569, note d.

Several expressions in this section bring to mind Luke's account of the Annunciation – "rejoice", "do not fear", "the Lord is in your midst".

Nahum

The single focus of Nahum is on the fall of Nineveh, which occurred just after, or even during, his prophetic ministry. As "one of the most eloquent orators in the Bible"[2] he harnesses his eloquence to a savage rejoicing over Assyria's destruction. His name "Nahum" may mean comfort or consolation, but the comfort and consolation he brings are for his long-suffering people. He underlines – even if one-sidedly – a message that runs through the Bible: God will judge and punish (as well as reward); evil will not finally triumph. The description of the Lord as "jealous and avenging" is an attempt to express his passionate concern not only for his own name, but also for the well-being of his people, and is coupled with the assurance that he cannot be indifferent to evil; if he is "slow to anger", that does not mean he will not finally intervene. His arrival is marked by "whirlwind and storm". His presence "dries up all the rivers". At his advance fertile areas wither, "mountains quake", "hills melt", "the earth heaves". And yet, for "those who take refuge in him", he is "good" and "a stronghold in a day of trouble". The Assyrians are warned that they will be defeated, their name forgotten, their idols thrown out, while the people of Judah are assured that the Lord "will afflict you no more"; he will "snap the bonds" of a century of Assyrian domination. A messenger will bring the "good tidings" and celebrations will mark the defeat of the old enemy. Even the northern kingdom will be restored (1:1 – 2:2).

The fall of Nineveh, under the combined assault of Babylonians and Medes, is vividly pictured: warriors appear, "clothed in crimson", bearing blood-red shields, riding on "chargers" or in "chariots" which "dart like lightning" through the city. The gates, battered open, are like a giant dam that has been breached; Nineveh sees its "waters [its people] run away", despite the order "Halt! Halt!" There is booty galore, silver and gold, and "no end of treasure". In the city there is only "devastation, desolation, and destruction", and "all faces grow pale". Assyria's deity, Ishtar, was often depicted as accompanied by a lion, and Assyria itself was lion-like in its treatment of others, filling its "dens with torn flesh". But now the lion roars no more; its dens are empty, its cubs destroyed: "the Lord of hosts" has declared, "I am against you" (2:3-13).

2 C. Stuhlmueller CP, *Amos, Hosea, Micah, Nahum, Zephaniah, Habakkuk: Collegeville Bible Commentary*, no. 15 (Collegeville, MN: Liturgical Press, 1986), p. 87.

The final chapter takes the form of a victory celebration over Nineveh, that "city of bloodshed", filled with plunder. There's a brilliant thumbnail sketch of an Assyrian army on the move: "The crack of whip and rumble of wheel, galloping horse and bounding chariot! Horsemen charging, flashing sword and glittering spear, piles of dead, heaps of corpses". In the face of such an army, any nation must have frozen with fear. "I am against you, says the Lord of hosts," and that means that Nineveh's fate is sealed. With a sneer, the Assyrians are asked: "Are you better than Thebes [former capital of Egypt]?" Everyone knew that Thebes, an apparently impregnable city, had fallen to the Babylonians. Now it is Nineveh's turn for destruction. Its fighting men will be like "women in your midst", its defences will be useless and the people will disappear like locusts which, warmed by the sun, rise in the air and fly away. The last words of this fierce book invite "all who hear the news" to "clap their hands" with joy (2:14 – 3:19).

> However much this book may surprise, or even shock, its essential message may still be a source of comfort and consolation (*nahum*) to people who live under an oppressive regime in any modern "Nineveh".

Habakkuk

This deeply reflective prophet ministered from about 605 (when Egypt was defeated by the Babylonians) to 587 (when Jerusalem fell to the same army). He grieves at God's apparent indifference to evil, especially that of the chosen people. He is the first prophet to challenge God directly over the apparent discrepancy between divine justice and the terrible injustices in this world. In doing so, he "makes an important and original contribution to the sum of Israel's reflection on the nature of its God and of God's ways with Israel".[3]

Habakkuk's first complaint is: "O Lord, how long shall I cry for help, and you will not listen?" There is "destruction and violence" everywhere, "the wicked surround the righteous" and wickedness prevails: why does God not intervene? The Lord's response is disconcerting: just as Assyria had been used as "the rod of my anger" (Isaiah 10:5) against his people, so now, he tells the prophet, "the Chaldeans" (the Babylonians) will be the instrument of his justice. And how fearsome they will be: "Their horses are swifter than leopards, more menacing than wolves at dusk... Their horsemen... fly like an eagle... they gather captives like sand... their own might is their god" (1:2-11).

---

[3] A.R. Ceresko, "Habakkuk", in R.E. Brown, J.A. Fitzmyer, R.E Murphy (eds), *The New Jerome Biblical Commentary* (London: G. Chapman, 1989), p. 261.

Habakkuk repeats his complaint: how can "my Holy One", with "eyes... too pure to behold evil", possibly allow "the wicked [to] swallow those more righteous than they [that is, the people of Israel!]?" In their ruthlessness the Babylonians show as little concern for their captives as fishermen do for their catch; they even offer sacrifice to their "net" (a reference to the armaments that won them their victories) (1:12-17).

The prophet stands "at [his] watchpost" awaiting the Lord's response, which, the Lord commands, is to be written in letters so plain that the message can be read on the run; and the people are urged to "wait for it" with patience. And this is the message: "the righteous live by their faith" (or, better, their faithfulness); they are loyal and enduring, but the arrogant are unstable, they "do not endure" (2:1-5).

A fivefold "woe" (translated "alas" in the NRSV) follows: the first tells how the Babylonians heap up the possessions of nations, as though they had been given them "in pledge", but the nations insist that they were loans, and now demand repayment. The second woe is against those who have tried to ensure the safety of their "house" (either their dwelling or their dynasty) by plunder and extortion. "The very stones" and "woodwork" cry out against them. Woe three is against those who build town and city at the cost of "bloodshed", though it ends with the promise, already given in Isaiah 11:9, that "the earth will be filled with the knowledge of the glory of the Lord, as the waters cover the sea". Woe four is a condemnation of those who get their neighbours drunk in order to humiliate them; they in turn will experience horrors at the hand of the Lord. The final woe is an indictment of idolatry: it pokes fun at the impotence of idols whose owners cannot get them to "wake up" in the morning, for "there is no breath in [them] at all". What a contrast between them and "the Lord... in his holy temple", before whom "all the earth" is ordered to "keep silence" (2:6-20).

A splendid psalm-like prayer brings the book to an end. It begins with a review of God's mighty deeds in the past and a plea that they may be renewed "in our own time". The Lord is visualised coming forth from the direction of Sinai – "Teman" lies to the far south and Mount Paran to the south-west of Jerusalem – and leading his people in the final stage of a journey from slavery in Egypt to freedom in the Promised Land. His appearance is marked by "brightness... like the sun", with "rays" flashing from his hands; it causes "the earth" to shake, "the nations" to tremble, "the eternal mountains" to be shattered. The victory, recorded in terms of a Canaanite myth about a god-like warrior who conquers the raging sea, sees the whole of nature – "mountains", "deep", "sun" and "moon" – responding in panic at the approach of the divine warrior who comes "to save [his] people" and finally tramples down "the sea". The prophet trembles at the thought of this awesome victory and the psalm ends with an amazing act of faith: no matter what may happen, though crops should fail and "the stalls" of the flocks lie empty, yet "I will rejoice in the Lord... exult in the God of my salvation", confident that he will make "my feet like the feet of the deer" so that I may "tread upon the heights", well out of harm's way (3:1-19).

In 2001 an epidemic of foot-and-mouth disease spread across the UK, leading to the slaughter of thousands of sheep and cattle, and threatening farmers and their families with financial ruin. Throughout the epidemic, a prayer group in the south of England, whose members all belonged to the farming community, would pray, each time they met, the final verses of Habakkuk, including the powerful words: "Though... the fields yield no food; though the flock is cut off... and there is no herd in the stalls, yet I will rejoice in the Lord..." Thus the prayer of a seventh-century prophet was movingly appropriate for Christians of the third millennium. It is still true that "the righteous live by their faith[fulness]" (2:4).

SECTION TWO
The Exile

The sixth-century prophets

When Jehoiakim (609–598 BC) makes the fateful decision to rebel against his Babylonian overlords, he brings upon Israel the most harrowing event in its history, though he himself is spared the tragedy: he dies while Nebuchadnezzar and his army are marching upon Jerusalem. The ensuing siege lasts for about three months, ending in 597 with the fall of the city, the looting of treasures from the Temple and the royal palace, and the leading into exile in Babylon of the new king, Jehoiachin (598), and the leading citizens. The Babylonians leave behind a puppet king, Zedekiah (597–586), uncle of Jehoiachin, but, when he too rebels, Nebuchadnezzar returns. This time the siege lasts two terrible years. The wall is breached in the summer of 587; Zedekiah is caught attempting to escape and a terrible fate awaits him: he is forced to watch – it is the last scene he will ever witness – the beheading of his two sons. Then, blinded by his captors, he, the last of the royal line of David, is taken in chains to Babylon. Jerusalem is razed to the ground, the Temple destroyed and most of the survivors herded into exile. Shortly after, Gedaliah, whom the Babylonians have appointed administrator, is assassinated by nationalists who want the restoration of the Davidic line.

Throughout this traumatic period, as well as the latter part of the previous century, the most powerful prophetic voice to be heard – though seldom heeded – is that of JEREMIAH. Like prophets before him, he begs the people to amend their ways, return to the demands of the covenant and put their trust in the Lord. If, as seems likely, he supports the religious reform initiated by Josiah, he has the disappointment of seeing it come to an end with Josiah's untimely death in 609, for the three kings – Jehoahaz, Jehoiakim and Jehoiachin – who succeed Josiah show no interest in upholding his ideals. The prophet sees the folly of rebelling against Babylon, but his warnings fail to deter the kings from such suicidal policy; and so the Babylonian exile begins.

It would be hard to exaggerate the feelings experienced by the Hebrew people as they trudge on the long, painful journey to Babylon. They carry into a pagan land vivid memories of the smoking ruins of Jerusalem and her Temple. One of them expresses their feelings in the memorable words: "By the rivers of Babylon – there we sat and wept…" (Psalm 137). Another records "your servants hold its [Jerusalem's] stones dear and have pity on its dust" (Psalm 102:14). The city was supposed to be under the Lord's protection.

What could her fall mean? For some it means that Babylon has a god who is stronger than the Lord, and so they renounce their faith. But for many others it has a very different meaning. "The classical prophets... had argued that the people's... fate [was] determined by their fidelity or infidelity to God... This understanding of history provided the means by which the people could now interpret first their tragic conditions and understand their fate as punishment from God rather than as an indication of the Lord's weakness. Thus they could remain faithful to their God even in the midst of calamity and even look forward to the future with some hope and expectation."[1]

If it is Jeremiah who presents this "understanding of history" in the days prior to the fall of Jerusalem and in the early days of the exile, there are two other major prophets who continue his work. The first, EZEKIEL, is among the deportees to Babylon after the earlier destruction of Jerusalem and spends his entire ministry among the exiles, spearheading a revival of spirit among them and inspiring them with hope for the future. The other, an anonymous prophet known as ISAIAH II (or Deutero-Isaiah), is a sixth-century disciple of Isaiah of Jerusalem and applies the teaching of the great prophet to the new situation. One of the major themes of his ministry, which begins towards the end of the exile, is that the Lord has not forgotten his people and that they will soon return to their own land in a second exodus. OBADIAH is another prophet of this period, but given the brevity of his book (twenty-one verses), the nature of its contents (a diatribe against Edom, which had rejoiced at Jerusalem's fall and taken advantage of it) and its absence from the liturgy, he need concern us no further.

The fulfilment of the promise of Isaiah II comes in 539, at the end of half a century of exile. Those years, far from being an unmitigated tragedy, prove in many ways to be a time of blessing: when faith grows stronger; when religious activity is intense; when Israel's traditions are gathered together and much of the Old Testament appears in the form it has today; when such "exclusive" Jewish practices as circumcision and sabbath observance are emphasised; when, in the absence of the Temple for sacrificial worship, it seems likely that the synagogue, a meeting house for prayer, scriptural readings and instruction, comes into existence.

The end of exile dawns in 539 when, after a meteoric rise to power, Cyrus, King of Persia (558–530), defeats the Babylonians and becomes ruler of the Middle East. In accordance with enlightened Persian policy, he authorises as many of the exiles as wish to return home, and there rebuild their city and her Temple. A new chapter in their history is about to begin.

---

[1] J. Maxwell Miller and J. Hayes, *A History of Ancient Israel and Judah* (London: SCM Press, 1999), p. 421.

7 Jeremiah
– seduced by the Lord

About one hundred years after the birth of Isaiah, another child was born near Jerusalem, who was destined to become one of Israel's most illustrious prophets. Jeremiah's long ministry, lasting over forty years, covered the best and worst of times. The best – when the religious reform initiated by Josiah was under way and it seemed the people would return to the Lord. The worst – when Josiah was killed, the people reneged on their promises, and, within the space of a decade or so, Jerusalem fell twice to Babylonian armies; and, on the second occasion, most of her people were carried off into exile.

Josiah's death in 609 BC and the waning of Assyrian power lulled many into a sense of complacency. With religious reform no longer in the air and the Assyrian threat removed, they felt they had nothing to fear from slipping back into the old ways. Jeremiah did not share the prevailing view that, since the Lord was in his Temple and had promised David an everlasting dynasty, the safety of Jerusalem was assured. He was convinced that the people's fate depended on their behaviour: covenant faithfulness had to be shown in their lives. He believed that as God had used Assyria to punish the northern kingdom a century earlier for its infidelity, so God would use Babylon to punish the southern kingdom for a similar reason.

It was a view that earned him enemies and put his life at risk. Nor were the enemies only from without; within Jeremiah's own heart there were fears and uncertainties, as becomes clear in a series of autobiographical passages – the "Confessions of Jeremiah" – in which he lays bare his frustrations and self-doubts. Why did a man of such obvious sensitivity adopt so thankless a ministry? The answer is to be found in the harsh, even shocking, title of this chapter; it was because, to use his own words, he was seduced by God.[1] He was an unwilling spokesman but had no doubt that he spoke in the Lord's name; it was that conviction that enabled him to persevere to the end.

Jeremiah's call

Jeremiah, son of the priest Hilkiah, was born at Anathoth, four miles north-east of Jerusalem. His ministry, which began in "the thirteenth year" of King Josiah's reign (626) – though some scholars believe that 626 was in fact the date of the prophet's birth – covered the reigns of Josiah and his successors, continuing until the fall of Jerusalem, and beyond. "The word of the Lord" revealed to him that even before his birth God "knew" him,

---

[1] Jeremiah 20:7 reads in NRSV: "O Lord, you have enticed me, and I was enticed."

"consecrated" him and "appointed" him prophet, and not only to Israel but even "to the nations", because the crisis of his people affected many others. Moses-like, Jeremiah protests: "I do not know how to speak, for I am only a boy." The Lord insists, "you shall go to all to whom I send you, and you shall speak whatever I command you", but he assures him, "I am with you", and, touching his lips, adds: "I have put my words in your mouth." Jeremiah's task is "to pluck up and to pull down, to destroy and to overthrow", but also "to build and to plant". The term "jeremiad", which has entered the English language, reflects the laments and warnings so often on the lips of Jeremiah. But there were positive aspects to his ministry, too – emphasis on the intimacy of our relationship with God, on the necessity of accepting personal responsibility, and on the new covenant to be struck between the Lord and his people. Some six centuries later, when Jesus spoke of the new and everlasting covenant in his blood,[2] the promise of this most courageous of prophets was fulfilled to an extent that he could never have imagined.

His call is confirmed by two events. First, he interprets the branch of "an almond tree" (*shaqed*) as an assurance that the Lord will be "watching" (*shoqed*) his word to ensure its fulfilment. Then, in "a boiling pot" tilting "from the north", he sees a sign of impending invasion by the Babylonians. (Babylon's armies have to skirt the desert to reach the city and so descend upon it from the north.) Jeremiah must "gird" himself for action, speak out boldly and stand firm. Strengthened by God, he will be resolute as "a fortified city", firm as "an iron pillar" and unshakable as "a bronze wall" (1:1-16).

Despite the book's notorious lack of chronological precision, it may be helpful to link various parts of Jeremiah's career to the reigns of particular kings.

Josiah (640–609): Jeremiah's earliest sermons, 2:1 – 6:30

"Return to me, faithless Judah"

The prophet's reproaches begin, like those of Hosea, with a reminder that the covenant relationship with Israel is like a marriage in which the Lord is the bridegroom and Israel the bride. Alas, the "devotion" and "love" of honeymoon days are over: the bride has reneged on her marriage vows and gone after other gods, forgetting the Lord who showed her such love, who "brought [her] out of Egypt", "led [her] in the wilderness" and brought

---

[2] The covenant of Israel is not superseded but rather achieves a new fulfilment, "that is, in a fundamental progressive continuity, which necessarily involves breaks at certain points. Continuity concerns above all the covenant relationship, while the breaks concern the Old Testament institutions that were supposed to establish and maintain that relationship. In the New Testament, the covenant is established on a new foundation, the person and work of Christ Jesus; the covenant relationship is deepened and broadened, opened to all through Christian faith" (Pontifical Biblical Commission, *The Jewish People and their Sacred Scriptures in the Christian Bible* [Vatican: Libreria editrice vaticana, 2002], §§39-40).

her into "a plentiful land". Such infidelity stands in marked contrast to the fidelity that pagans show their gods – "even though they are no gods" at all. Not only have God's people forsaken God, "the fountain of living water", they have chosen pagan gods, "cracked cisterns that can hold no water". They have besported themselves "on every high hill" (where Baal worship regularly took place). The Lord had planted his people "as a choice vine" (see Isaiah 5), but they have become "degenerate". The behaviour accompanying Baal worship is like that of a she-camel in heat, desperate to find a partner. They have made cult symbols gods, but gods that never help (2:1-37).

Again in language reminiscent of Hosea, Jeremiah speaks of the Lord's yearning for the return of his faithless bride – but not a return at any cost: Judah must repent. A divorcee, who has remarried and then left her second husband, may not return to the first: she has made herself unacceptable to him (see Deuteronomy 24:4). Similarly, Judah has defiled the very land by her unfaithfulness, and yet brazenly shows not the slightest shame; she even has the hypocrisy to go on calling upon the Lord as, "My Father… the friend of my youth". "Faithless Israel [the northern kingdom] has shown herself less guilty than false Judah."

Nonetheless, the Lord cannot conceal his longing. He will do what no human husband would do: receive back his erring wife, provided only that she repents. "Return, O faithless children," he pleads, "and I will bring you [back] to Zion." They will have leaders "after my own heart", the two kingdoms will be reunited and Jerusalem will be a centre for "all nations". But the return must be genuine: they must live according to covenant ideals – "truth… justice, and… uprightness". An inner conversion is called for, circumcision of "the foreskin of [their] hearts" (3:1 – 4:4).

"Give heed to the sound of the trumpet"

This moving portrait of a grieving God, yearning for the return of his unfaithful bride, now gives way to a more sombre picture of a God not to be mocked, a God warning and threatening his people. The sound of "the trumpet" of war proclaims that an invading army is near. All are urged to seek refuge behind fortified walls, while the enemy is likened to a lion about to pounce. Jerusalem may be the holy city, but she cannot claim immunity from attack, for the threatening Babylonian army is the instrument of the Lord's anger. Neither king nor priest nor prophet is equal to this occasion; they have constantly led the people astray, assuring them that the city was impregnable, that "It shall be well with you." The swift, all-conquering advance of the invaders is graphically pictured in terms of a powerful storm from the desert and then of a "whirlwind". Even now the prophet seems to offer the possibility of a reprieve if only the people will "wash [their] heart clean of wickedness" (4:5-14).

But already it may be too late: heralds in the north of the country are passing word to Jerusalem that an invading army is on its way. Jeremiah reveals his own anguish as he contemplates the fate of his beloved people, and the Lord sadly responds: "my people… do not know me… are skilled at doing evil, but do not know how to do good". What is to happen will be like the dissolution of creation: earth and heavens reduced to their primal "waste and void" with panic-stricken people scrambling for safety "among rocks". Meanwhile, bold Jerusalem decks herself in her finery and, like the prostitute she is, tries to woo the invaders! Finally, she is pictured as a vulnerable woman crying out in childbirth, but the cries are not for a birth but the fall of the city (4:15-31).

The Lord invites the prophet to scour Jerusalem to see if he can find even "one person who acts justly". Some may call upon the Lord, but it is all hypocrisy: "they have refused to turn back". Such callous disobedience is found not only among the unschooled in "the law of their God", but also among those who ought to know better. They will be torn to pieces as if by wild animals "because… their apostasies are great". Allied to unfaithfulness to God is unfaithfulness in their marital relationships. They imagine that the Lord will not intervene, but he assures them: "I am going to bring upon you a nation from far away", an army "whose language you do not know", "mighty warriors" who will "eat up" all they hold dear and destroy "your fortified cities". There are times when it seems that the Lord cannot bear to destroy his people totally: "I will not make a full end of you," he declares. Nonetheless, the people have eyes and ears but fail to see or hear, have "a stubborn and rebellious heart" and do not fear the God of creation. The land is scarred by social injustice and oppression of the poor; the leadership, whether of prophet or priest, is valueless. "Where covenant with the Lord is betrayed, covenant values in social relationships cannot be sustained."[3]

The trumpet of war sounds again to the south of Jerusalem. The enemy may think they plan the strategy, but it is the Lord who is organising it. The inhabitants will face the harvesting of the Lord: houses, fields and wives too, handed over to others; God's hand will stretch out not to save but to destroy. The leaders, with their false notions of the impregnability of the city, continue to speak of "peace" and the people fall for the propaganda. Even when the Lord begs them, "Stand at the crossroads, and look… where the good way lies," their response is, "We will not walk in it"; and when

---

[3] W. Brueggemann, *A Commentary on Jeremiah* (Grand Rapids, MI: Wm B. Eerdman's Publishing Co., 1998), p. 71.

called upon to give heed to "sentinels" (prophets), they respond: "We will not give heed." Their fate is sealed; empty ritual will not save them. Once more the warning is given of a cruel and merciless army, "coming from the land of the north". People are paralysed with fear; a disaster, terrible as the loss of "an only child", is about to befall them. Jeremiah sadly admits that he is like "a tester" of precious metal; the outcome of his investigations is that Israel is like dross that can only be discarded (5:1 – 6:30).

Jehoiakim (609–598): 7:1 – 20:18

The Temple Sermon

This is a key event in the life of Jeremiah. Obeying "the word… from the Lord", he goes to the Temple entrance. The people see God's presence in the Temple as a guarantee that they will be kept safe, that the promises about the royal city are unconditional, independent of their behaviour. Not so, roars the prophet; in a stark message, he declares that, without amendment of life, the endlessly repeated slogan, "This is the temple of the Lord", will not save them. They must amend their lives, and that means that they "act justly with one another", "do not oppress the alien, the orphan, and the widow", do not "shed innocent blood in this place", and "do not go after other gods". Otherwise, exile awaits them.

Jeremiah sees little likelihood that they will amend their ways. They transgress the commandments that are at the heart of the covenant and then have the hardihood to come into the Temple, perform liturgical rituals and tell themselves: "We are safe!" So the Temple is turned into "a den of robbers", where those who flout the covenant can safely hide. Angrily, he compares Jerusalem to Shiloh. Everyone knew that the temple at Shiloh had been the centre of Israel's worship and that it had been destroyed by the Philistines because of Israel's disobedience. Since Jerusalem was just as disobedient, she would earn herself a similar fate. Speaking in God's name, Jeremiah declares: "I will do to the house that is called by my name… what I did to Shiloh." It is too late for Jeremiah to intercede for the people: too late, because "the towns of Judah" are steeped in worship of false gods, such as "the queen of heaven" (probably the Mesopotamian goddess, Ishtar); too late, because their "burnt offerings" are a hypocritical smokescreen; too late, because what is required is obedience and they refuse to obey. The Lord will withdraw his protection and they will face disaster, with widespread slaughter; the bodies of those once honoured in the city will be disinterred and exposed to "the sun and the moon", the heavenly bodies they once worshipped. Death will seem preferable to life. For this speech, which was greeted with cries of treachery and blasphemy, Jeremiah will pay dearly (7:1 – 8:3).

"For the hurt of my poor people I am hurt"

He continues his invective, though more in sorrow than in anger. Normally, he says, when people fall they pick themselves up, when they go astray, they turn back, but not God's people: they sin but are unrepentant, they rush into evil "like a horse plunging headlong into battle". Even the birds know when to come and go; it's natural for them. But the Lord's people behave unnaturally, not recognising that their well-being depends upon return to covenant living. The leaders have led the people astray so that they are like a vineyard or fig tree that fails to produce fruit. Now they must prepare for a siege. Invasion is coming from the north in the shape of fearsome cavalry, and along with them pollution of the water supply and wholesale terror.

The prophet speaks movingly of his distress at "the cry of my poor people". He longs for their healing: "Is there no balm in Gilead [renowned for its healing properties]?" he cries, well knowing that nothing can ease their plight; he could weep "day and night". Torn between love for them and horror at their infidelity, he longs to get away and be free of their deception and violence. Their only cure is "to know… the Lord", but they lack that knowledge (in Hosea's sense of the word). There is nothing to be done now except "weeping and wailing": Jerusalem is going to be reduced to a "heap of ruins", devoid even of cattle and birds. To the question how such widespread devastation can be justified, the Lord answers: "Because they have forsaken my law." A public dirge is announced: "mourning women" are invited to raise a dirge over the ravaged land and the bodies of the dead. Death is envisaged creeping burglar-like through windows, making its way even into royal palaces and destroying the youth, the hope for the future.

Neither wisdom nor might nor wealth can save the people, says the Lord, but only the covenant virtues – "steadfast love, justice, and righteousness". Circumcision will not help if they remain unresponsive to the Lord; they are no better than idol-worshippers, whose handiworks, "like scarecrows", are unable to "speak", "walk" or "do evil" – or "do good"; they are "foolish" (*hebel* = nothingness, vanity), no matter how their makers adorn them. In contrast, "the Lord is… the living God and the everlasting King"; he brought all things into being; he is the Lord of history and "Israel is the tribe of his inheritance".

In a poem perhaps dating from when the Babylonians were actually besieging Jerusalem, Jeremiah tells the people to pack their bags and prepare for exile. He expresses his grief at what is to happen and prays that the punishment will be in proportion to the weakness of "human beings" rather than to their objective wickedness.

He warns "the people of Judah and the inhabitants of Jerusalem" that a curse lies upon "anyone who does not heed the words of this covenant". At Sinai, disobedient Israel suffered the consequences. Now their descendants "have turned back to the iniquities of their ancestors… they have gone after other gods", and so the Lord "will not listen to them" when they cry out. They may seek the help of their newfound gods, but will discover it's a waste of time. No prayer or ritual offering will save them, for they have provoked "me to anger by making offerings to Baal" (8:4 – 11:17).

The "Confessions"

Between chapters 11 and 20 stand the five "Confessions" of Jeremiah, outpourings that reveal his frustration, distress and bewilderment. They have been described as "the most direct, candid, and intimate prayers… in the OT"[4] and "central for the interpretation of Jeremiah".[5]

He speaks of his anguish that "the people of Anathoth", his native village, are plotting against him, intent on killing him if he keeps on prophesying; he is "like a gentle lamb led to the slaughter". He raises the age-old complaint: why do the evil prosper and, by implication, the just (like himself) suffer? His enemies should be treated to the medicine they have prepared for him. The only reply from the Lord is that what is to come will be so much worse than what has been: it will be like comparing the speed of a human runner with that of a horse. It's no real answer; Jeremiah must be content to trust (11:18 – 12:6).

In inner crisis, he regrets that he was born; he is "a man… of contention to the whole land". The people cannot abide the message and so have turned on the messenger; and yet he has interceded for them so faithfully that the Lord had to ask him to desist! God's word has been "the delight of [his] heart"; he has been unswerving in loyalty, yet the Lord has been as deceptive as a "brook" that holds no water. "Why", he cries, "is my pain unceasing?" He is told that if he will "turn back" in deeper fidelity, he will be "a fortified wall of bronze"; his enemies will yield to him, and the Lord will say, "I am with you to save" (15:10-21).

He pleads that it will not be he who is "shamed" or "dismayed", but his "persecutors". Only then, he seems to say, will the Lord be vindicated as a God of justice (17:14-18).

---

[4] Brueggemann, *Commentary on Jeremiah*, p. 114.
[5] G. von Rad, *The Message of the Prophets* (London: SCM Press, 1967), p. 173.

Again he speaks of his horror at the plots his enemies are hatching. They "have dug a pit for my life". Indignantly, he pleads with God to "give heed to me", and asks whether evil is all the recompense he gets for the good he has done. He did intercede for the people; now he begs that every misfortune may befall them, that they may never be forgiven. As Jeremiah sees it, they have become God's enemies and, unless they are dealt with, the Lord's honour will be impugned (18:19-23).

Jeremiah is revealed at his most despairing: the mission entrusted to him has been costly almost beyond endurance. He accuses the Lord of seducing him, with the result that "I have become a laughing-stock all day long". Whenever he opens his mouth, it is to shout, "Violence and destruction!" He has even been tempted to speak no more "in his name", but then "within me there is something like a burning fire", and he cannot hold it in. A whispering campaign has been orchestrated against him; even "close friends" wait for him "to stumble", mockingly naming him "Terror is all around" – in other words, Jeremiah spells trouble. Then, quite unexpectedly, the prophet speaks of his trust in the Lord, who stands beside him "like a dread warrior" so that it is not he but his persecutors who "will stumble". Since the Lord sees "the heart and the mind", he confidently asks that he and his adversaries may receive their due reward. He even bursts into a song of praise for what he is sure the Lord will do. But then, as though overwhelmed at the thought of his plight, he curses, in a manner "unique in the prophetic literature",[6] "the day on which I was born" and the messenger who brought news of his birth to his father. "Why", he asks, "did I come forth from the womb to see toil and sorrow and spend my days in shame?" Why had the Lord laid upon him such a mission? The questions remain unanswered (20:7-18).

As a background to these "Confessions" there is the constant account of the people's unfaithfulness and of the terrible fate that awaits them. Wickedness has become endemic, so that to ask Judah to change her ways is like asking "Ethiopians [to] change their skin, or leopards their spots" (13:23)! Judah's guilt is indelibly engraved, as though with an iron, diamond-tipped pen, on "the tablet of their hearts", as well as on the altars set up for Baal worship (17:1). We also learn how, in accordance with "the word of the Lord", he is to remain unmarried. Wifeless and childless, he is a living symbol of the disaster soon to befall Jerusalem (16:1-2).

On two occasions he dramatises his message by a symbolic action. First, he hides a linen loincloth in "a cleft of the rock" near the river Euphrates

---

[6] James M. Ward, *Thus Says the Lord* (Nashville: Abingdon Press, 1991), p. 138.

– when he retrieves it later it is "ruined"; and so too, he explains, are the people. They were meant to cling to the Lord as closely as a person's garment to their body, but have torn themselves away; the Lord "will not pity or spare or have compassion" (13:1-14).

Secondly, in the shop of a potter, he notes how, when a pot turns out misshapen, the potter reworks it "into another vessel". It's a parable of the Lord's freedom to behave in similar fashion with his people. Unlike the clay, they have the power to choose, but their choice is: "We will follow our own plans" – a recipe for disaster. As surely as "the snow of Lebanon" is a permanent feature of the lofty crags, as surely as mountain streams run downwards, so, just as surely, Israel should cling to the Lord. But it has forgotten him, worshipped "a delusion", and so its people will be scattered into exile, and "I [the Lord] will show them my back". Then, together with the community's leaders and carrying "an earthenware jug", Jeremiah goes to the Potsherd Gate at the south end of the city and proclaims a frightening word from the Lord of disaster for the city. Finally, he shatters the jug: "So", says the Lord, "will I break this people... as one breaks a potter's vessel." The reaction of Pashhur, the chief priest, is to have Jeremiah beaten and placed overnight in the stocks. Far from being intimidated, the moment his humiliating treatment is over, he boldly warns Pashhur that the Lord has given him a new name: "Terror-all-round"! It is not peace but terror that the Temple now stands for. For the first time, he explicitly identifies Babylon as the enemy that will destroy Jerusalem, plunder her Temple and lead her people, including Pashhur and his family, into exile: "to Babylon you shall go; there you shall die" (18:1 – 20:6).

Zedekiah (597–586): 21:1 – 45:5

Judgement on Jerusalem, her kings and prophets

When Jerusalem fell to Nebuchadnezzar in 597, the Babylonians deported King Jehoiachin and placed his uncle Zedekiah on the throne. But he proved less compliant than they had hoped; and so in 588 they renewed the siege of the city. Zedekiah sends representatives to Jeremiah, hoping the prophet will have an encouraging word for him and that the Lord "will perform a wonderful deed" to match those of the past. The prophet's response is: not only will the Lord not protect them, but the "outstretched arm and mighty hand" that brought them out of Egypt will now bring the Babylonians into Jerusalem; they can still choose between "the way of life and the way of death", the latter for those who stay in the city and resist the invaders, the former for those who surrender to the "Chaldeans" (Babylonians). There is a warning for the kings of the "house of David": unless they act with justice, protect "the alien, the orphan, and the widow" and refrain from shedding innocent blood, the royal house will become "a desolation". Jerusalem, encompassed by valleys, is called "inhabitant of the valley" and, perhaps in reference to the mount on which its Temple stands, "rock of the plain"; but it will become "an uninhabited city". When passers-by from other nations ask what brought this about, the answer will be: "they abandoned the covenant of the Lord their God, and worshipped other gods". Josiah's sons – Shallum (Jehoahaz) and Jehoiakim – are indicted as unworthy of their father. Because of the hopes pinned on him, Josiah was regarded as "the signet ring" on God's right hand, but the ring would be torn off: no child of his would ever sit on the throne of David. Similarly, Jehoiakim's son Coniah (Jehoiachin) is rejected and will face exile in Babylon.

After this condemnation of "the shepherds" for their neglect of the sheep, leading to the scattering of the flock, there suddenly appears, like a shaft of light piercing dark clouds, a series of promises from the Lord: "I myself will gather the remnant of my flock out of all the lands" (of exile) and "bring them back to their fold"; and, in words reminiscent of Isaiah 11:1, "I will raise up for David a righteous Branch" (king) who will practise "justice and righteousness"; and finally the Lord will perform a "wonderful deed" – liberation from exile in Babylon will outshine the wonder of the Exodus. As suddenly as the bright light of hope had appeared, the dark clouds gather once more. Jeremiah launches another attack, this time levelled against false prophets. He had "announced the end of Judah's 'known world'. The (false) Prophets... tried in various ways to soften the massive judgment he anticipated."[7] Jeremiah expresses his dismay at the harm they are doing; even the land suffers as a result. Their ungodly behaviour is more appalling than that of the prophets of the northern kingdom, and they will be punished accordingly. What they say does not come "from the mouth of the Lord" but from their own imagination, which is distorted by the conviction that the Lord will always protect king and Temple. According to ancient mythology, God presides over a council of the heavenly court and messengers relay important messages to earth. Jeremiah claims to be such a messenger, but God tells the false prophets: I did not send you; I did not speak to you. Genuine revelation comes through God's word, which is "like a hammer that breaks a rock in pieces" (21:1 – 23:40).

Good figs and bad

Jeremiah has a vision of two baskets, one full of "very good figs", the other of "very bad figs". The good figs represent those exiled to Babylon: "I will set my eyes upon them for good", and "I will bring them back... I will give

---

[7] Brueggemann, *Commentary on Jeremiah*, p. 207.

them a heart to know that I am the Lord; and they shall be my people and I will be their God." But the bad, uneatable, figs are those remaining in Jerusalem, because they stand in contradiction to God's plans, and so can expect "sword, famine, and pestilence". In the words of one commentator: God seems "to *make* the future with those whom the world judges to be *without* a future"[8] (24:1-10).

Babylon has been master of the Middle East and a constant threat to Israel for over twenty years. Jeremiah reminds the people that they have consistently rejected his preaching, and so the Lord is going to bring Babylon "against this land and its inhabitants"; its leader will be "my servant" and Israel will be utterly destroyed. The sounds of mirth, even the sounds of everyday life, will be heard no more and the nation will face "seventy years" (that is, a long, indefinite time) of exile (25:1-38).

Jeremiah faces hostility and encourages the exiles

Jeremiah opposes popular belief in the impregnability of Jerusalem, contending that the city's only chance of survival lies in conversion to the covenant, and that the Babylonian menace is God's judgement upon city and people. In a kind of flashback, we are transported to Jeremiah's famous speech against the Temple in chapter 7 and learn of its repercussions: the religious leaders want the king to have the prophet executed. With enormous courage, Jeremiah replies: "I am in your hands. Do with me as seems good." In the ensuing dispute, it is pointed out that when the prophet Micah said much the same as Jeremiah it had led not to his death, but to the people's repentance and the city's reprieve. (Admittedly, another prophet, Uriah, who spoke against the city was less fortunate!) Jeremiah is in real danger; and only the intervention of an influential family in the city saves him (26:1-24).

Back again in Zedekiah's reign, shortly after the first invasion of Jerusalem in 598, Jeremiah publicly wears a yoke to symbolise Babylonian domination, declaring that the rulers of surrounding nations must all submit to the yoke of Babylon, according to the will of the Lord who has sovereignty over all peoples; but Babylon's rule will ultimately come to an end. Zedekiah soon hears the message, as do the priests. Jeremiah urges the people not to listen to prophets who are "prophesying falsely" that the sacred vessels ransacked from the Temple will soon be returned; not only will they not be returned, but the rest of the treasures will be taken away to Babylon too (27:1-22).

---

[8] Brueggemann, *Commentary on Jeremiah*, p. 220.

Hananiah confronts Jeremiah: claiming to speak in the name of the Lord, he tells the people that "the yoke of the king of Babylon" is broken, that within a couple of years the sacred vessels and all the exiles will come home. Would that that might be so, retorts Jeremiah. Hananiah seizes hold of Jeremiah's yoke and breaks it, a dramatic reiteration of his claim that the Lord will break the yoke of Babylon. But Jeremiah has the last word: he explains that the yoke of exile is made of iron; it cannot be broken. Within twelve months Hananiah is dead – but there is no end to the exile (28:1-17).

Aware that even among the exiles there are those who claim that they will soon be home, Jeremiah sends a letter, promising that those who accept exile positively will find that God is at work in their midst. He pleads with them: "Build houses and live in them; plant gardens and eat what they produce. Take wives and have sons and daughters... seek the welfare of the city where I have sent you [says the Lord]." Then Jeremiah opens up the astonishing prospect of an eventual homecoming: God can still do the unexpected, for God's plans are "for your welfare and not for harm" and "give you a future with hope". And "if you search for me with all your heart, I will let you find me... and I will bring you back". There are harsh threats for false prophets in Babylon, and also for king and people who remain in Jerusalem imagining they are God's favoured ones. Both groups "would not listen" to the Lord, and both will experience the familiar trio of sword, famine and pestilence, and their city will become "a derision among all the nations". The implication is that not only will there be another invasion, but the city will face dissolution. Two false prophets in Babylon are warned that they will suffer a violent death at the hands of the Babylonians and become a byword among the exiles. Finally, there is an indictment of Shemaiah, who had written to the priests in Jerusalem, urging them to take action against Jeremiah because of his letter to the exiles. However, the priest who received the message shared its contents with Jeremiah and took no further action (29:1-32).

"The Book of Comfort"

Once more "the word" of the Lord comes to the prophet: he is to "write in a book all... that I have spoken to you. For the days are surely coming... when I will restore the fortunes of my people... and... bring them back." This is a message of much-needed comfort for the exiles who in anguish clutch their stomachs like women in childbirth. God is still powerfully at work: the God who willed exile now wills homecoming. The God who plucks up and tears down is the God who will plant and build (cf. 1:10). "Exile is not a defeat or failure for God, but the arena out of which God works a glorious newness for God's beloved people and for God's treasured city."[9]

---

[9] Brueggemann, *Commentary on Jeremiah*, p. 270.

The Lord's promise is that Israel "shall be rescued", the yoke broken, and God's people, no longer servants of other nations, will "serve the Lord their God" and a Davidic king. Despite divine assurances – "have no fear", "do not be dismayed", "I am going to save you", "I am with you" – Israel's condition is likened to that of an incurable "wound". There is only one cure for the incurable – the "compassion" (literally, the mother-love) of God. "Your wounds I will heal"; "the city shall be rebuilt"; out of it will come forth "the sound of merrymakers"; and a ruler will come "from their midst" and "you shall be my people, and I will be your God". Only "in the latter days" – when the Babylonian empire has been destroyed – will they finally understand what has happened; in the meantime they must live by faith.

They will find "grace" in "the wilderness" of exile, just as their ancestors found it in the desert, and will discover that "I have loved you with an everlasting love" and that "my faithfulness" is enduring. "Again" the Lord will build up the nation, "again" there will be music and festivity, and "again" planting and harvesting, and the Temple will be restored. As "the remnant of Israel" is brought home, the presence of many who are weak and vulnerable will highlight the miraculous nature of the new Exodus. Like a loving father, the Lord will care for them on their homeward journey; like a shepherd, he will gather and protect them. Faces will be "radiant over the goodness of the Lord". Young and old will rejoice. Rachel, wife of Jacob and mother of Joseph, is pictured weeping at Ramah (a northern town "resited" close to Bethlehem by a later tradition [cf. Matthew 2:18]) over her children taken into captivity, "because they are no more". But the Lord tells her: "your children shall come back". They have struck their "thigh", a gesture of shame, and will return – by the way they went into exile – assured, as the Lord's "dear son", of forgiveness. Now "a woman encompasses a man": there is "a resumption of the loving relationship between Israel and her husband, the Lord".[10] Sion is once more the meeting place for the Lord and his people. It will be like a dream come true. As the Lord kept a watchful eye on the negative aspects of Jeremiah's mission – the plucking up and breaking down – so he will do the same for the positive – the building and the planting. Many exiles felt they were suffering for those whose wickedness led to the fall of Jerusalem, and so a bitter proverb had been coined: "The parents have eaten sour grapes, and the children's teeth are set on edge." But the prophet insists on personal responsibility – on the part of individuals and of generations.

The people have shown an inability to keep the covenant and have brought disaster upon themselves, but now the Lord will take the initiative. "The

---

[10] *The New Jerusalem Bible*, ed. H. Wansbrough (London: Darton, Longman & Todd, 1985), p. 1349, note h.

days are surely coming… when I will make a new covenant with the house of Israel and the house of Judah." The covenant of Moses was primarily a relationship between God and the nation; this one, written on the human heart, will also be a relationship between God and each individual member of the community. God's law will be interiorised; it will no longer be written on "tablets of stone" but "on their hearts" and will result in ready obedience. The covenant has not been superseded but rather has achieved a new fulfilment,[11] made possible by the gratuitous pardon of the Lord. Now the possibility of their being rejected by him is as unthinkable as the collapse of the "fixed order" of sun, moon and stars, or the ability (by the standards of Jeremiah's day) to measure the heights and depths of the cosmos. Jerusalem will be rebuilt and again "be sacred to the Lord". Even while Jerusalem is surrounded by the Babylonians, Jeremiah ostentatiously buys a field in his hometown of Anathoth – an act of faith in the Lord's promise to restore his people to their own land.

The final chapter of this section consists of promises the Lord makes to Jeremiah while he is a political prisoner "in the court of the guard": first, despite the fearful troubles the people have brought on themselves by "their wickedness", the Lord "will restore… Judah and… Israel", "rebuild them", "cleanse them from all the guilt of their sin"; and the now desolate cities and towns of Judah will be alive with "the voice of the bridegroom and the voice of the bride" and songs of thanks to the Lord, "for his steadfast love endures for ever"; and "the nations of the earth" will be amazed at the transformation. Second, there is a promise, reaffirming that a "righteous Branch" will "spring up for David" (cf. 23:5-6), and, as sure as day follows night, Israel will never be deprived of a Davidic king. For those who still doubt, the Lord gives the absolute assurance: "I will restore their fortunes, and will have mercy" (30:1 – 33:26).

Fidelity and infidelity – obedience and disobedience

Jerusalem is facing an onslaught from Nebuchadnezzar, "all his army… and all the peoples under his dominion". Only two other cities of Judah now remain, and Jeremiah announces that Jerusalem will fall; the king will be taken to Babylon and meet a terrible fate. The king is assured, however, that if he will "hear the word of the Lord" – and submit to Babylon – he will die in peace and be appropriately honoured. It was probably when the siege of Jerusalem was lifted as the Babylonian armies turned to stem an advance

---

[11] The expression "new covenant" is not found elsewhere in the Old Testament, but Ezekiel 36:26 develops the idea by announcing the gift of a "new heart" and a "new spirit". At the Last Supper Jesus made his blood "the blood of the new covenant", recalling the ratification of the Sinai covenant by Moses and suggesting continuity with it, but also a radical newness, for Christ's covenant is founded on the blood of a human being who transforms his death into a generous gift (cf. Pontifical Biblical Commission, *The Jewish People and their Sacred Scriptures in the Christian Bible*, §§39, 40).

of Egyptian forces that Zedekiah granted Hebrew slaves their freedom, in accordance with Deuteronomy 15:12; but when the siege was resumed, king and nobles reneged on the agreement. In striking contrast to their dishonesty is the story of the Rechabites, radical Israelites who followed the ascetic lifestyle of the first followers of Moses. When, in King Jehoiakim's time, they sought protection within the city walls, they were offered wine, but refused to drink out of obedience to their founder. The prophet contrasts their obedience to a human ancestor and Israel's disobedience to the Lord himself. The Rechabites will be blessed, but not his own countrypeople unless they learn a lesson from them (34:1 – 35:18).

The last days of Jeremiah

(This section, known as the Baruch Document, begins in chapter 36 with an account of how Baruch, Jeremiah's secretary, wrote a scroll dictated by the prophet and ends in chapter 45 with a promise of blessings for him.)

The year is 605. Jehoiakim is king and Jeremiah has become a marked man. No longer welcome in public, he calls upon his secretary to write in a scroll at his dictation "all the words of the Lord that he had spoken to him", perhaps a summary of his preaching thus far. Then he is sent to read the scroll to the people in the hope that they "will turn from their evil ways". Obediently, Baruch goes to the Temple and performs his duty; brought before the authorities, he is made to read the scroll to them. They advise Baruch and Jeremiah to go into hiding and meanwhile inform the king. As he in his turn listens to the scroll, he shows his contempt by feeding the document piece by piece to the fire and orders the arrest of Jeremiah and Baruch. Jeremiah's response is to dictate the scroll again and add a searing condemnation of the king (36:1-32).

When the Babylonians lift the siege on Jerusalem in order to confront the Egyptians, Zedekiah sends to ask Jeremiah to pray for him. The grim message brought back from Jeremiah is that the Egyptians will retire, the Babylonians will return and Jerusalem's fate is sealed. Jeremiah tries to take advantage of a lull in the siege to return home to Anathoth, but is arrested as a deserter, beaten up and thrown into prison. The king calls him to the palace secretly and anxiously enquires: "Is there any word from the Lord?" There is; but again not one the king wants to hear: "You shall be handed over to the king of Babylon." He does, however, have Jeremiah transferred to a more humane prison in "the court of the guard".

News of Jeremiah's preaching – he has greater freedom in his new gaol – reaches the officials. Appalled that he is encouraging people to surrender to the Babylonians as their only hope and even as the Lord's will, they brand him a traitor and, with the king's tacit approval, have him lowered into a miry cistern, where he is left to die. But Ebed-melech, an Ethiopian servant of the king, persuades his royal master to let him go. With help, he hauls Jeremiah out of the pit, thoughtfully easing the operation for the prophet by placing cloth pads under his armpits. Hardly is Jeremiah free than the king again arranges a secret rendezvous in the hope of receiving a message from the Lord. At first, fearful for his life, Jeremiah is reluctant to say anything. Only when Zedekiah swears to protect him does he give the dreaded message: surrender to the Babylonians and "your life shall be spared, and this city shall not be burned"; refuse to surrender and neither king nor city will escape. Not even Jeremiah's vivid description of what will happen when the city falls can persuade Zedekiah to follow his advice. But he does enter into an agreement that neither of them will reveal to court officials the nature of their conversation. With that, Jeremiah returns to his prison in the court of the guard – to remain there till the fall of Jerusalem.

Jeremiah's threats are realised in 587 when, after an eighteen-month siege, the city walls are breached and Jerusalem falls to the Babylonians. Zedekiah, trying to make his escape by night, is quickly apprehended, taken to Nebuchadnezzar's field HQ in Syria and, after the slaughter of his sons, blinded and taken to Babylon. Having got rid of the royal household, the Babylonians plunder the city, torch palace and Temple, and lead many of the people into exile. Jeremiah fares better, benefiting from the advice he has so often given others – "submit and all will be well"; on the orders of Nebuchadnezzar, he is allowed unharmed to choose where to live. He chooses the home of Gedaliah and to stay "with his own people". He is also able to assure Ebed-melech that his life will be spared. Gedaliah, appointed governor of Judah, lives a few miles north of Jerusalem. Some people regard him as a stooge of the Babylonians. Informed that Ishmael, one of Judah's royal house, who had fled to Ammon to escape the Babylonians, is now plotting to kill him, he refuses to believe it. The refusal costs him his life: Ishmael and his companions slay Gedaliah and, after the motiveless murder of a band of pilgrims to Jerusalem, make their escape.

The people and military leaders, fearing that once they hear of Gedaliah's murder the Babylonians will take reprisals, resolve to flee to Egypt, but decide to consult Jeremiah first. They promise to "obey the voice of the Lord our God". The prophet advises that they stay in the land and have no fear of the king of Babylon; and also warns that if they go to Egypt they will meet with disaster and none of them will survive. But the decision has already been taken: dismissing Jeremiah's word as "a lie", they set off for Egypt, taking the prophet and Baruch with them, and settle in an Egyptian border fortress. There, Jeremiah again performs a symbolic action. He makes some large stones into the foundation for a throne near the entrance to the Pharaoh's palace, explaining that the throne is intended for Nebuchadnezzar! He "shall pick clean the land of Egypt, as a shepherd picks his cloak clean of vermin", and so will catch up with those who disobeyed the Lord.

Jeremiah's final plea is addressed to exiles living in various Egyptian cities. They have followed the example of their brothers and sisters in Jerusalem, "making offerings to other gods", and will be punished. They retort that in fact they did well when they practised idolatry; it was when they stopped in Josiah's reign that one disaster followed upon another! Jeremiah warns that the Pharaoh, on whom they depend, will be handed over to his enemies, just as Zedekiah was handed over to Nebuchadnezzar. These are the last recorded public utterances of an extraordinary prophet, who died far away from home, to the end bearing witness to the Lord whom he had served so courageously for forty years. There is a final private word of encouragement for Baruch, his trusty secretary: he is assured that though the Lord will "break down… and pluck up" all that has been built and planted, at least Baruch's own life will be spared (37:1 – 45:5).

Oracles against the nations

Such oracles seem particularly appropriate on the lips of one appointed to be "prophet to the nations" (1:5). The violent language is the exaggerated, stylised, speech of the day. Jeremiah's concern is to show that the fate befalling Israel's enemies is proof of the Lord's sovereign power; he shares the psalmist's view: "Why should the nations say: 'Where is their God?' Let the avenging of the outpoured blood of your servants be known among the nations before our eyes" (Psalm 79:10). The Lord is not to be mocked.

Egypt, the only power capable of standing up to Babylon, suffered a crushing defeat at the hands of Babylon at Carchemish: once "rising like the Nile" in its pride, it was forced into headlong retreat. As there was no healing balm from Gilead for Israel so there is no healing for Egypt. Its major cities destroyed, its god leaves the field of battle in shame, while the Pharaoh is compared to a bully boy who fails when put to the test. But "my servant Jacob" is assured, "I will not make an end of you!" (46:1-28).

Several of Israel's traditional enemies are singled out: first, the Philistines who live on the Mediterranean coast will fall to Babylon, as her armies move south, like "an overflowing torrent"; then Moab, to the east of the Dead Sea, whose chief cities are doomed and whose god, Chemosh, will be sent into exile together with priests and princes; like wine, which a lazy winemaker has not troubled to separate from the lees, complacent Moab has remained undisturbed, but now the time for decanting has come! She who treated Israel as "a laughing-stock" will be repaid and everywhere there will be signs of grief – shaving of heads and beards, lacerating of hands, wearing of sackcloth. Yet even now the final word is a word of hope: "I will restore the fortunes of Moab" (47:1 – 48:47).

Brief oracles threaten five other nations. First, the Ammonites, to the north of Moab, whose land "shall become a desolate mound". Second, Edom, to the south of Moab, will suffer a terrible fate: a grape-gatherer does not pick the vine clean, even a robber leaves something behind, but the Lord's destruction of Edom will be total. Third, Syria, with its capital Damascus, lying to the north-east of Galilee, is facing disaster. Fourth, Kedar and its Bedouin people who live far to the east, who felt so secure that they had no gates or bars to halt an enemy, will be scattered and have their possessions taken as booty. And fifth, Elam, standing in the plains lying to the east of Mesopotamia, will be destroyed and the sword will follow its people until they finally acknowledge the Lord's rule (49:1-39).

The final oracle, spread over two complex chapters, deals with Babylon, Israel's enemy par excellence. It had been constantly in Jeremiah's thoughts and in his preaching, and finally it brought disaster upon Jerusalem. But now comes the incredible announcement that Babylon too stands under divine judgement: it will be wiped off the map and its gods put "put to shame"; and this means the return of the exiles, northerners and southerners alike, who will "come weeping [to Jerusalem]… and join themselves to the Lord by an everlasting covenant that will never be forgotten".

Meanwhile the usual taunts and victory songs over a defeated enemy are heard, followed by an extraordinary poem to "a sword" that will destroy Babylon's people, its warriors, its horses and chariots, its treasures, its water supply. What Babylon visited upon others will now be visited upon Babylon. It may once have been the Lord's "golden cup", used to punish other people, but now it "is shattered" and is warned, "your end has come". In contrast to idol-makers, "the Lord of hosts" has power and wisdom of cosmic proportions, and he is on the side of "Israel… the tribe of his inheritance". A poem, like that of the sword, sings of a "war club" with which the Lord smashes (repeated no less than nine times!) the enemy so thoroughly that Babylon is reduced to "a perpetual waste". Relays of messengers announce the news: the "city is taken". Bel the god of the Babylonians may have swallowed up Jerusalem, but now will be made to disgorge "what he has swallowed"; and the exiles are exhorted to "remember" that Jerusalem is their true home and so leave the city of Babylon. And who guarantees all this? "The King, whose name is the Lord of hosts."

The final "words of Jeremiah" report that he wrote an account of the disasters that would befall Babylon and commanded Seraiah, who accompanied Zedekiah into exile, to read it publicly and then tie a stone to it and throw it into the Euphrates – Babylon is to sink and rise no more (50:1 – 51:64).

Historical appendix

Chapter 52 (cf. 2 Kings 25) recapitulates the story of Jerusalem's fall, and the ensuing wholesale exile that left behind only "some of the poorest people of the land to be vinedressers and tillers of the soil". The chapter ends with news that Jehoiachin, a hostage in Babylon, was released and treated as a royal personage "up to the day of his death". Many, in Babylon and in devastated Judah, regarded him as their legitimate king, so his release left them a glimmer of hope. Thus, the chapter hints that just as the prophet's threats of Jerusalem's fall have been realised, so his promises of an eventual end to exile will be realised also.

However, when that happened, Jeremiah was not among those returning to Jerusalem. It is not known when he died; but his influence continues to be felt. His immense courage and commitment to God's call, his resolution despite bitter opposition, sufferings and bouts of self-doubt, have made this loneliest of prophets a type, a foreshadowing, of Jesus himself; and when Jesus' disciples were asked who people thought Jesus was, it is fascinating to learn that some thought he might be Jeremiah returned.

Ezekiel
– exiled with the exiles

With Ezekiel, son of Buzi, we enter the world of exile. He was probably among the first batch of Judaean prisoners deported to Babylon after the siege of Jerusalem (597 BC), and was the first prophet to receive his call while living outside his native land. His twenty-two-year ministry, it seems, was spent in Babylon, at Tel-abib, on the banks of the river Chebar, which served as an irrigation canal between the Euphrates and the city.

The exiles were overwhelmed as they left their homes and material possessions behind and made the long, painful journey to Babylon on foot. With the fall of Jerusalem in 587, another batch of exiles arrived; they came from a gutted city, and a devastated Temple and royal palace. Altar and throne gone, they must have felt God had abandoned them. In supporting his fellow exiles Ezekiel didn't encourage self-pity: more vigorously than Jeremiah, and apparently with less personal anguish, he denounced sin and warned of its consequences. This is the main thrust of his preaching until the city actually fell (chapters 1–24). Later his words were more comforting, and he ends with a utopian vision of a restored Temple in a renewed Jerusalem amidst a holy people, faithful to a new covenant (chapters 25–48).

Like Amos, Ezekiel insisted on the need for justice. Like Hosea, he compared Israel to an unfaithful wife. Like Isaiah, he was awed by the ineffable holiness of God and deeply concerned for the Temple. Like Jeremiah, a slightly older contemporary, he came from a priestly family and taught that the future lay with the exiles, whom he saw as the nucleus of a renewed people of God. But despite similarities, Jeremiah and Ezekiel were "extremely different not only in temperament, but especially in their way of thinking, speaking and writing".[1] Ezekiel was given to expansive discourses, strange allegories, bizarre acted-out parables and spectacular visions: his style might be described, in architectural terms, as baroque. If "prophesying… lends itself to generalization and oversimplification… [n]owhere in the prophetic literature is this tendency carried further than in Ezekiel".[2]

He delivers powerful messages about personal responsibility; about the need for a renewal involving not simply a "circumcised heart", as Jeremiah taught, but a new heart; about the new covenant that the Lord will strike with his people; about the Lord as good shepherd to his people and God of all the nations; and about the worldwide saving role of Israel. He is not

---

[1] G. von Rad, *The Message of the Prophets* (London: SCM Press, 1967), p. 189.
[2] James M. Ward, *Thus Says the Lord* (Nashville: Abingdon Press, 1991), p. 192.

only a priest and a prophet but "a theologian as well",[3] playing a major role in the founding of Judaism.[4] Notable features in the book of Ezekiel are: its autobiographical form; its series of dates – more than a dozen – from the start of his career (593) to the restored Temple (571); and its four magnificent visions, which highlight key events in the unfolding story and will serve as milestones on our journey.

First great vision and call of Ezekiel

In 593 Ezekiel saw "a great cloud", wheeling in from the north, edged with brightness and emitting tongues of flashing fire; in the midst of its amber-coloured heart, he saw four strange creatures, each human in form with feet like those of a calf; each had four wings and four faces – that of a human being, a lion, an ox and an eagle. (They have become Christian symbols of the four evangelists.) When the creatures' wings flapped, it sounded "like the thunder of the Almighty"; two wings modestly covered the body of each and two linked the four creatures together, while flaming torches moved to and fro between them. Beside each there was what seemed "like a wheel within a wheel" with rims "full of eyes all around"; its ability to move in every direction suggested God's omnipresence. Above a crystal dome stood a throne on which sat "something that seemed like a human form", though only the upper part of the body was clearly visible. The scene was bathed in light, like the colours of the rainbow, and had "the appearance of the likeness of the glory (*kabod*) of the Lord". This "glory", signifying the presence of God's unapproachable majesty, assumed a luminous human form. The cautious language – "something like", "something that seemed like", and so on – suggests an attempt to describe the indescribable. And what is impossible to describe is also impossible to visualise! But Ezekiel the priest has no difficulty in recognising its significance: the Lord's "glory", associated with the Temple in Jerusalem, is now appearing in the midst of the people in exile; the Lord, on his mobile chariot-throne, is in their midst, and Ezekiel falls prostrate before him.

A voice, addressing him as "mortal" (son of man), bids him stand and prepare to receive a message. The title "mortal", underlining his fragility in comparison with the towering majesty of God,[5] will appear more than ninety times. As Isaiah was appointed in a vision of the Almighty, so Ezekiel receives his commission in similar fashion, and, like Isaiah, is told that he is

---

[3] Von Rad, *Message of the Prophets*, p. 173.
[4] "Judaism": the word is derived from "Judah" and refers to practices that were prominent during the exile, such as emphasis on Torah, circumcision and the sabbath, and also perhaps to the beginning of the synagogue. All served as coping strategies for a traumatised people.
[5] The Hebrew expression "son of man" is synonymous with "human being". In the prophecy of Daniel it is used of the Messiah and in the New Testament of Jesus.

to prophesy to a nation that will not be receptive: it will be like living amid "briers and thorns" and "scorpions". But, whether they hear or not, "they shall know that there has been a prophet among them". Then he is offered a scroll on which are words of "lamentation and mourning and woe" and is told to eat it. When he does so, he finds, as Jeremiah did (Jeremiah 15:16), that God's word is "as sweet as honey". However, though he shares a common language and common tradition with the people, their hardness of heart will be an insurmountable barrier. Nevertheless Ezekiel must continue to proclaim: "Thus says the Lord God" (1:1 – 3:15).

The initial vision ends with the sound of the wings and wheels of the departing chariot of the Lord. Meanwhile, Ezekiel is whisked to the exile settlement of Tel-abib. After initial exultation, he sits "stunned" for seven days.[6] The Lord announces that he is to be "a sentinel for the house of Israel". If he warns and his hearers ignore it, he is acquitted of all responsibility, but should he fail to warn, he must pay the price; on the other hand, not only the wicked who fail to respond but also the righteous who return to evil will "surely die". Life-and-death language is appropriate in this context, for, like a soldier in wartime, Ezekiel's fate and his people's are inextricably linked. The prophets were passionate and expressed themselves in passionate terms – no one more than Ezekiel. In trying to highlight the appalling nature of the people's sins, he seems to delight in their misfortunes and attributes to God a vindictiveness that has more of the human than the divine about it (3:16-21).

Mimes and messages of judgement

After the week of immobility, Ezekiel is commanded to proceed to "the valley" and there the vision of the "glory of the Lord" opens up again. Lifted up by the spirit, he learns that he is to remain at home, speechless and bound with cords, and to illustrate the fate of Jerusalem by performing symbolic actions that will "enhance the force of the spoken word".[7] First, on a clay brick, he is to sketch a picture of Jerusalem under siege and set his "face toward it", mimicking the Lord's unwavering hostility. Second, he is to lie for a number of days first on one side, then on the other, signifying the years the northern and southern kingdoms, respectively, will endure the nightmare of exile. Third, acting like one of the besieged, he is to weigh out carefully the meagre rations of grains and water allotted for each day. Finally, he is to divide the hair of his head and beard into three parts, and

---

[6] NRSV translation is perhaps misleading: Ezekiel's "experience is described as a state of ecstatic elation… succeeded, as is psychologically plausible, by a period… during which he remained… in a catatonic state" (J. Blenkinsopp, *Ezekiel* [Interpretation series; Louisville, KY: John Knox, 1990], p. 28).
[7] Blenkinsopp, *Ezekiel*, p. 34.

dispose of it in a way that illustrates the horrors that will follow the firing of the city by the Babylonians. The few strands of hair kept in the prophet's cloak represent the remnant that will remain faithful to the Lord.

The theme of punishment to be inflicted upon Jerusalem continues. The chosen city has betrayed the Lord and so must pay the penalty. War, pestilence and famine will drive people to cannibalism. Jerusalem will become "an object of mocking among the nations". The prophet delivers two fearful sermons. He sets his face – again a symbol of irrevocable hostility – but this time "toward the mountains of Israel", in particular the "high places" desecrated by pagan worship. Altars and incense-stands will be destroyed and "the corpses of the people [scattered]… in front of their idols". And they "shall know that I am the Lord". Survivors, taken captive to far-away lands, will "remember" their covenant obligations and how "their wanton heart… turned away from me". The prophet gives dramatic intensity to his threats by claps and stamping: the people face sword, famine and pestilence; the land will be a desolate waste "from the wilderness" in the south "to Riblah" in the north. "Then they shall know that I am the Lord."

The second sermon is addressed to "the land of Israel", as the former was addressed to its mountains. For the people, the land was more than a piece of territory: it gave them significance as a people. The message to the land can be stated in two words – "the end" – repeated time and again: "The end has come… Now the end is upon you… See, the day!" Perhaps Ezekiel has in mind "the day of the Lord" (Amos 5:18), the day of divine retribution. The characteristic events of normal social living will disappear: there will be no point in buying and selling, in winning or losing a deal, in hoarding silver and gold. "The sword is outside, pestilence and famine are inside." Those who escape will flutter "like doves" to the mountains. No one will respond to the trumpet call to arms: soldiers' hands will hang limp, their bladders out of control through fear, and their heads shaven as in mourning. "My treasured place" (the Temple) will be profaned by the Babylonians. In their desire for peace, people will consult prophet, priest and elder, but there will be no prophetic utterance, no priestly instruction and no counsel from the elders. The section ends with a final declaration of the purpose of these dreadful events: "they shall know that I am the Lord" (3:22 – 7:27).

Second great vision: the Lord leaves the Temple

"In the sixth year [592], in the sixth month, on the fifth day", the prophet is sitting at home "with the elders" when suddenly he falls into a trance as "the hand of the Lord God fell upon" him. A mysterious figure (an angel?) transports him to the Temple, where he proceeds towards the northern wall by stages, each stage revealing "greater abominations" and increasing the grief felt by Ezekiel, a priest filled with awe of God's holiness. First, stationed in the gateway is "the image of jealousy", perhaps a statue of the fertility goddess. Second, after passing into a room in the wall, Ezekiel sees paintings of loathsome creatures and the seventy elders of Israel, censers in hand, engaged in idol worship. Third, at the entrance of the north gate, women lament the annual departure of the spring god Tammuz. Finally, the vilest abomination of all: in front of the Temple a group of men turn their backs and set their faces towards the east, as they prostrate themselves before the sun; then they put "the branch to their nose", perhaps an obscene gesture directed towards the Lord. In response the Lord warns: "my eye will not spare, nor will I have pity".

Sentence is carried out immediately: six "executioners" appear, "each with his weapon… in his hand", to be joined by a scribe "clothed in linen". The seven executioners represent the city's total destruction. Then "the glory of the God of Israel" moves from the Holy of Holies to station itself at the Temple entrance, while the scribe passes through the city marking with "X" (Hebrew *tau*) the foreheads of all who are uncontaminated by idolatry. The rest of the group follows, slaughtering indiscriminately those who do not bear the mark. Despite Ezekiel's prayer, the Lord insists: "I will bring down their deeds upon their heads." Finally the scribe reports that the Lord's command has been carried out. Then Ezekiel witnesses another vision of the throne chariot and its four creatures (here called "cherubim", like the angels whose outstretched wings protect the ark of the covenant); with live coals taken from their midst, the city is torched. The "glory of the Lord" fills the Temple a last time before being carried off in the cherubim chariot amidst fire and clouds: the Lord is abandoning his apostate people.

Meanwhile, twenty-five royal counsellors recommend that Zedekiah should continue the fight against Babylon, perhaps with the aid of Egypt. They compare the situation in Jerusalem to that of meat in a cooking pot. Ezekiel's response is that though they may escape "the pot" by fleeing the city, the sword will catch up with them. Before the prophecy ends one counsellor is dead, and Ezekiel cries out: "Lord God! will you make a full end of the remnant of Israel?" To those in the city who claim that the exiles have deserted the Lord and lost their right to the land, Ezekiel explains that in their exile the Lord has "been a sanctuary for them" and eventually will bring them back home, with hearts transformed so that they will abide by the covenant. Once more "they shall be my people, and I will be their God". Finally, "the glory of the Lord" moves from the east gate across the Kidron valley and stops on the Mount of Olives, before returning to Babylon, while Ezekiel is brought back to rejoin the exiles (8:1 – 11:25).

Inevitability of Jerusalem's fall

Many remain unconvinced by Ezekiel, but he insists that Jerusalem will face disaster. The Lord complains that the people "have eyes... but do not see... ears... but do not hear" and commands Ezekiel to perform "in their sight" actions that will symbolise their fate: he is to pack his belongings and, in the middle of the night, dig through the wall of his house and, with face covered, hasten into the darkness. This is how the people will be carried into exile and King Zedekiah taken sightless and shackled into captivity. But the Lord promises, "I will let a few of them escape." Ezekiel's second symbolic action is to eat and drink "with quaking", simulating the panic of the inhabitants of a city under siege. The people respond that prophecies go unfulfilled, or if they are fulfilled, it is at a much later date, but the Lord replies that this prophecy will be fulfilled – and without delay.

Ezekiel turns his attention to "those who prophesy out of their own imagination". They say what their hearers want to hear, crying, "'Peace' when there is no peace". They are like people daubing a wall with whitewash to give it the appearance of solidity, but "a deluge of rain" is enough to show up their handiwork for what it is. A similar condemnation falls upon female prophets – sorcerers or witches – who resort to magical practices and promise to bring good or bad fortune to those who trust them.

Again the elders come to consult Ezekiel, but he discerns that they are not sincere and warns that instead of receiving a prophetic word they will encounter God in person; the same will be true of anyone consulting a prophet while taking "idols into their hearts". Both the prophet and the one consulting the prophet will be cut off "from the midst of my people", a fate tantamount to a death sentence. If the Lord's "deadly acts of judgement" should befall the city, the "righteousness" (*sedeqah*) even of the proverbially holy ones, "Noah, Daniel, and Job", would not stave off disaster. Behind these words lies the doctrine of personal responsibility to which Ezekiel will return. Again, the Lord declares that there will be survivors – "a remnant" (12:1 – 14:23).

Allegories of judgement

Israel is like a dead vine whose only value is as firewood; the Lord is about to consign Jerusalem to the flames. A lengthy allegory compares the city to a faithless wife. Jerusalem was an orphan, cast aside by her parents (as many children were in ancient times) on the day of her birth. The Lord, passing by, rescued the tiny abandoned child. When she reached "the age for love" he "spread the edge of [his] cloak over [her]", a sign of his intention to marry her, showered her with gifts, and she grew "exceedingly beautiful, fit to be a queen". This parable records the Lord's choice of Israel, despite her insignificance, and his entering into a covenant with her. But, alas, the story does not end there. Jerusalem becomes so enamoured of her beauty and forgetful of the Lord that she resorts to a life of promiscuity. Adultery was a traditional way of referring to Israel's unfaithfulness: it took the form of involvement in cults that included ritual prostitution and, worse still, human sacrifice. This unfaithful and homicidal wife will be stripped, stoned by the mob and cut to pieces, while "many women" (that is, other nations) will look on. Never again will she be unfaithful and so the Lord's wrath will be satisfied. Jerusalem's behaviour has been worse than that of her two "sisters", Samaria and Sodom, but they and Jerusalem, together with "her daughters" (neighbouring cities), will find forgiveness, though Jerusalem will retain an abiding sense of shame. Finally, in a passage added after Ezekiel's time, the Lord graciously reminds Jerusalem of the covenant struck with her "in the days of your youth" and promises to re-establish "an everlasting covenant". The violent imagery of this chapter is the prophet's way of helping his people to see the true nature of their evil conduct, while highlighting, by way of contrast, the extraordinary mercy of the Lord (15:1 – 16:63).

Another allegory follows, reflecting the political situation of the time. It's "a riddle", teasing the reader/hearer to think through its implications. Its interpretation is clarified by a point-by-point explanation: a "great eagle" (Nebuchadnezzar) descended upon Judah in 597 and broke off "the top of the cedar" (King Jehoiachin) and carried it off to "a land of trade" (Babylon). It then took "a seed from the land" (Zedekiah, who replaced his nephew on the throne) and, once planted, it grew into a luxuriant vine; but it made the fatal mistake of stretching out towards "another great eagle" (Egypt, whose aid Zedekiah sought), and the vine (Judah) withered in the searing "east wind" (God's anger, Babylon being its instrument). The tragedy is due to Zedekiah, who broke not only his oath to Nebuchadnezzar but also his covenant with the Lord. But the allegory ends with words of hope: the Lord will take "a sprig from the lofty top of a cedar", plant it on a mountain and care for it until it becomes a great and noble tree. Then "all the trees [other nations] shall know that I am the Lord", the only one with power to bring low the high tree and raise high the low one (17:1-24).

It was commonly believed among the exiles that they were suffering for their ancestors' wrongdoing, so that there was no possibility of their making a fresh start. It was a view encapsulated in the proverb, "The parents have eaten sour grapes, and the children's teeth are set on edge." Like Jeremiah, Ezekiel will have none of it; he insists that each person will be judged by his or her own actions. By way of illustration, he tells of a father, son and grandson. The first does what is right and "shall surely live" (enjoy association with God and the happiness it brings); the second, ignoring his father's good example, chooses to behave badly – "he shall surely die" (forfeit that association with God); the third, ignoring his father's bad example, behaves well – "he shall surely live". There is no carry-over, then, of good or evil from one generation to the next: we are moral agents who must take personal responsibility for our actions. Furthermore, should the wicked turn away from their wickedness, "they shall surely live"; and should the righteous turn to wickedness, "they shall die". And so instead of giving in to fatalistic notions, the people should hear the Lord's call to repentance and attain to "a new heart and a new spirit". In the meantime, just as each individual, so each new generation can decide its own destiny, choose its own future.[8] And so the Lord's call is: "Turn, then, and live" (18:1-32).

Ezekiel's literary skill is further highlighted by the double allegory of the lioness and of the vine. It has a melancholy air, befitting a lament on the passing of Israel's monarchy. The lioness is Judah; her two cubs, the last of Judah's kings, are Jehoahaz, who after three months' reign was taken to Egypt and died there, and (probably) Jehoiachin who, again after a brief reign, was exiled to Babylon where he remained for the next thirty-seven years. In the second allegory the vine is Jerusalem, "fruitful and full of branches"; her "strongest stem" (shoot), Zedekiah, last of Judah's kings, rebelled after ten years and "was plucked up in fury" and "transplanted into the wilderness" of Babylon (19:1-14).

The end is nigh

When once more elders from Judah gather at Ezekiel's house, he reveals "the word of the Lord", a damning survey that shows Israel has always been unfaithful. Time and again the Lord forgave them, "for the sake of my name": "Israel exists not for itself but to fulfil the divine purpose in history. That is why Israel must sanctify the name."[9] Ezekiel sees Israel's unfaithfulness stretching back to their time in Egypt; it was then, he says, that they defiled themselves "with the idols of Egypt". There never was a time when they lived up to the obligations of their relationship with the Lord. And so the Exodus was not so much liberation from slavery as break with idolatry.

Then the Lord "brought them into the wilderness". But instead of being the honeymoon period Hosea spoke of, it was in fact a time when the people rejected the Lord's statues and ordinances and sabbaths, and children chose to follow the bad example of their parents. Ezekiel even speaks of God giving them "statutes that were not good and ordinances by which they could not live", including, it would seem, child sacrifice! Perhaps the meaning of this

---

[8] W. Brueggemann, *A Commentary on Jeremiah* (Grand Rapids, MI: Wm B. Eerdman's Publishing Co., 1998) p. 291.
[9] Blenkinsopp, *Ezekiel*, p. 88.

mysterious statement is that the people interpreted as of God what in fact had been copied from other nations or what their own wicked hearts had devised (20:1-26).

Only a few verses are devoted to the six centuries and more that separate Israel's settlement in the land from the birth of Ezekiel, but the story is the same: involvement in pagan worship, frequenting of high places, child sacrifices. But this time there is no escape from God's wrath. Like a powerful king, "with a mighty hand and an outstretched arm", he will lead them in a new exodus into the desert where they will face the prospect of "face to face" judgement with the Lord. He will make them "pass under the staff" (like a shepherd checking his sheep), separating "the rebels" from the rest and never allowing them to return home. Possibly the purpose of the elders' meeting with Ezekiel had been to suggest the setting up in Babylon of an alternative centre of worship to the Temple, together with the cult of deities other than the Lord. They are warned: "What is in your mind shall never happen – the thought, 'Let us be like the nations… and worship wood and stone.'" Not until the rebellious element has been dealt with will the faithful remnant be gathered and brought back to "my holy mountain", Jerusalem, where they will be reconciled and make sacrifices pleasing to the Lord. The passage ends with the powerful announcement: "you shall know that I am the Lord, when I deal with you for my name's sake" (20:27-44).

Once again "The word of the Lord came" to Ezekiel. He is told to "set your face [in that hostile glare we met earlier (4:3)] toward the south" and warn that the Lord is to start a forest fire, spreading from "south to north" and destroying green wood and dry. When the prophet is mocked as "a maker of allegories", the Lord tells him to repeat the warning in unequivocal terms: he is to set his face precisely against Jerusalem and her sanctuaries, and announce that the Lord will destroy "both righteous and wicked", every soul from "south to north". He is broken-hearted and, when people ask why he moans, he tells them that their fate is sealed. An ominous passage describes a sword being sharpened and polished, ready "to be placed in the slayer's hand" and do its deadly work. Meanwhile there is wailing, striking of the thigh (a gesture of grief), a clapping of hands (as accompaniment to the thrusting action of the swordsman?), and Ezekiel himself, apparently, is told to brandish a sword. The people have despised the rod of God's discipline, now they must face the sword of the enemy (20:45 – 21:17).

As on a previous occasion Ezekiel performs symbolic actions to underline his message. He traces on the ground the outline of a road junction and a signpost, the latter's arms pointing in one direction to Rabbah, capital of Ammon, and in the other to Jerusalem. Nebuchadnezzar is to decide which direction he will take. After seeking divine guidance by various divinations, he marches upon Jerusalem, where battering rams and siege-towers will be used against the city. The people may make light of pagan divination practices, but the Lord has acted through them to achieve his purpose. Jerusalem will be attacked, the people will be "taken in hand" for their transgressions, particularly Zedekiah, referred to not as king but as "vile, wicked prince of Israel". A threefold repetition of "a ruin" expresses the chaos that will occur in Jerusalem. (Even then there is the enigmatic promise "until he comes whose right it is", a possible reference to the Messiah.) Finally, the language of the sword song is heard again, this time in reference to the Ammonites: a sword is being polished for them, too (21:18-32).

The corruption of Jerusalem and its citizens is denounced in three discourses, each headed with the familiar refrain: "The word of the Lord came to me." The first charges "the princes of Israel" and all who live in the city with involvement in bloodshed and idolatry, leading to contempt for parents, ill-treatment of orphans and widows, idolatry, neglect of the sabbath, bearing false witness ("bribes to shed blood"), incest and other kinds of lewd behaviour. All is summed up in the reproach that they "have forgotten" the Lord. The second compares Israel to scrap metal which after experiencing "the fire of [the Lord's] wrath" is reduced to a heap of valueless dross. And the third points out that the lack of cleansing rain upon the land is linked to their wickedness: princes, priests, prophets and the people themselves have failed in their respective duties (22:1-31).

Ezekiel continues his fierce indictment of Jerusalem with an allegory not unlike that of chapter 16, and in language just as outrageous. Samaria (capital of the northern kingdom) and Jerusalem (capital of the southern kingdom) appear under the names Oholah and Oholibah, respectively. They are sisters, each trying to outdo the other in wickedness. Both, says the Lord, "became mine" and so their unfaithfulness, their seeking help from foreign alliances (whether with Egyptians, Assyrians or Babylonians), is likened to adultery and prostitution. Both are whores, promiscuous even from the early days in Egypt. The northern kingdom tried to win the favours of Assyria and the final consequence was that she was attacked and abused by her former "lovers" and her people taken into exile (721 BC). Oholibah (Judah) behaved even worse than her sister: not content with one paramour, she hunted after several – seeking the help of Assyria, submitting to Babylon under the last of her kings, and finally, "remembering the days of her youth", turning again to Egypt and entering into alliances during the final days of the southern kingdom She will suffer at the hands of her lovers: the Babylonians, the Assyrians and tribes from the Babylonian empire. They will so mutilate her that, no longer desirable, she will be left naked and bereft. Like her sister, she will drink the "cup, deep and wide" of the wrath of the Lord. Finally, Ezekiel recapitulates the allegory, recounting the sins and warning that in the punishment that will follow they are to recognise the hand of their Lord. Then "you shall know that I am the Lord God" (23:1-49).

If the description of enemies gathering round the adulterous women is a picture of a city under siege, the picture is further clarified in a final allegory. Ezekiel is commanded to "write down" the precise date (588) which marks the beginning of the end for Jerusalem, as the armies of Nebuchadnezzar close in. Then he is to tell the people an allegory in which Jerusalem is compared to a boiling pot. On an earlier occasion the officials had boasted of the impregnability of Jerusalem, but now Ezekiel warns that the pot is going to be heated to the point of destruction for all inside. The Lord utters a double woe upon "the bloody city": the blood it has shed, and which clings rust-like to the sides of the pot, cries to heaven for vengeance. More logs are to be piled under the pot until it glows with the heat, and pot and contents perish. The Lord warns: "I will act. I will not refrain, I will not spare, I will not relent" (24:1-14).

About this time, Ezekiel learns of a terrible personal tragedy: the Lord tells him that suddenly ("with one blow") he is to lose his wife, "the delight of your eyes". Though he may "sigh" ("but not aloud"), he is to display none of the customary forms of grief: no public weeping or sprinkling of his head with ashes, no going barefoot or veiling his lower face, no sharing in a funeral meal. He gives the news to the people and the same night his wife dies. When they seek an explanation, Ezekiel tells them that in his personal tragedy he is a symbol of what is to happen to them: the Temple, "the delight of your eyes", will be desecrated and their compatriots whom they left behind in the city will be destroyed. But there is to be no show of grief, for no mourning could be an adequate response to the unbearable tragedy. Rather, they must discern in it the Lord's mysterious purpose; even in this event "they shall know that I am the Lord God" (24:15-24).

The final verses recall that Ezekiel remains silent until the day a messenger arrives in Babylon, reporting that the Temple has indeed been sacked. The first part of Ezekiel is now over, the second will not be taken up for several chapters.

Against the nations

Oracles against enemy nations, a feature of other prophetical books, occupy eight chapters in Ezekiel, sandwiched between the beginning of the siege of Jerusalem (chapter 24) and the report of its fall (chapter 33). They were delivered at different times but are gathered together, perhaps to show that divine judgement against Israel is balanced by divine judgement against the nations that brought about Israel's fall; the Lord is Lord of all the nations.

Ammon, Moab and Edom (running down the east side of the river Jordan) were related to Israel and are accused of taking advantage of Jerusalem's fall to ravage the land and even support Nebuchadnezzar. God will bring destruction on them by foreigners coming from the east. A fourth nation, Philistia, on the edge of the Mediterranean, is another traditional enemy that took advantage of Judah's defeat and will suffer defeat in its turn.

In contrast to these brief threats, a diatribe almost three chapters long is launched against Tyre, chief city of Phoenicia, situated on an almost impregnable island (today a peninsula) about a mile off the coast of Lebanon. It opposed Babylon before 587, but exulted over the fall of Jerusalem because it meant the end of a powerful commercial rival. It is warned that Nebuchadnezzar and his armies will sweep down upon Tyre like waves buffeting the land until it is reduced to "a bare rock", fit only for the nets of fishermen.[10] Its fall causes consternation among princes in surrounding cities. Despite power, wealth and culture, Tyre will no longer have a place in "the land of the living" but will descend into "the Pit" of the netherworld where "the people of long ago" are gathered.

In a magnificent allegory Tyre is compared to a huge ship, beautifully fitted out; planks of her sides from Senir (Mount Hermon); mast from a Lebanese cedar; oars from "oaks of Bashan"; deck, inlaid with ivory, from Cyprian pines; sails of Egyptian linen and awnings of "blue and purple" from Elishah (Cyprus?). Her crew comes from various Phoenician cities and "all the ships of the sea" come to barter for her wares. But hardly has the good ship Tyre reached the high seas than disaster strikes. She is overwhelmed by a powerful east wind and goes down with all hands on board. From round about people come down to the shore to perform mourning rites and lament over the tragedy, for Tyre has "come to a dreadful end and shall be no more for ever". Attention switches to "the prince of Tyre", for, though human, he has exalted himself as a god, and will pay the price: "strangers", in

---

[10] The siege lasted thirteen years and ended without much advantage to the victor. The radical destruction was accomplished only later, by Alexander the Great (*The New Jerusalem Bible*, ed. H. Wansbrough [London: Darton, Longman & Todd, 1985], p. 1437, note e).

the persons of the soldiers of Babylon, will be God's instruments to punish him. His collapse will be like a fall from paradisal splendour. There is a final brief oracle against Sidon, the other great Phoenician city, lying some twenty miles further north, and then an assurance that surrounding nations will no longer trouble Israel, like "a pricking brier or a piercing thorn", and that deportees will finally be set free and return home (25:1 – 28:26).

If the condemnation of Tyre was lengthy, that of Egypt is lengthier still, made up of seven oracles. Oracle One announces that Ezekiel is to "set [his] face against Pharaoh". It is 587; Pharaoh Hophra, compared to a crocodile sprawling in the Nile delta, is accused of claiming that the Nile is his: "I made it for myself." His fate will be like that of a crocodile dragged from the water and left stranded on the beach as the food of bird and beast. And, like fish clinging to its scales, his people will share his fate. When Judah sought Egypt's help, it was relying upon a staff made of reeds: the staff splintered and wounded the user. Now the sword will reduce Egypt to desolation, from northern Migdol to southern Syene. When the Lord restores it, it will be "a lowly kingdom" confined to the upper reaches of the Nile.

Oracle Two, dated 571, declares that Babylonian soldiers, unsuccessful in their assault on Tyre, lost the loot that would have been theirs, but now Nebuchadnezzar, as the Lord's agent, will conquer Egypt and reward them. The section ends with a promise of the coming of a Davidic ruler, and of Ezekiel's vindication.

Oracle Three announces "the day of the Lord is near" for Egypt and her allies. There will be universal desolation, the advance of Babylonian armies, the destruction of cities, a warning that the Lord will dry up the Nile and that never again will there be "a prince in the land of Egypt".

Oracle Four tells how in 588, just before the fall of Jerusalem, Pharaoh Hophra's troops had tried to raise the siege but were forced to withdraw. So depending upon Egypt is pointless: Pharaoh's defeated army is a broken arm, which has not healed, and should Egypt try to stop Nebuchadnezzar again, the other arm will be broken – by the Lord!

Oracle Five, dated 587, likens Pharaoh and his people to "a cedar of Lebanon". Among Lebanon cedars renowned for their height and solidity, this cedar is unique: it is even "the envy of all the trees of Eden". And yet, because of its arrogance, it will be toppled by "the most terrible of the nations" (Babylon) and descend into Sheol; all nations are to learn the lesson from "Pharaoh and all his horde".

The final oracles come from after the fall of Jerusalem. Oracle Six warns that though Pharaoh may have strutted like "a lion among nations", in fact he is a crocodile that the Lord will catch in a net, drag to land and leave as carrion meat. There will be cosmic consequences: the sky will be darkened and all nations will be appalled. It is Babylon that will "bring to ruin the pride of Egypt" and mourning women from all nations will join in the lament.

Oracle Seven proclaims that Egypt is to go down to the deepest depths of the underworld, its only consolation being that other great nations – such as Assyria, Elam and Edom – are already there. Pharaoh and his people will dwell, shamefully, "with the uncircumcised" (29:1 – 32:31).

Words of hope after fall of Jerusalem

Jerusalem's fall was a traumatic event for the people but a turning point for Ezekiel. Earlier, his ministry had been a continual warning of tragedy to come. The night before news reaches him that "the city has fallen",[11] the Lord opens Ezekiel's mouth, making him ready for his ministry of hope and reconciliation. As if to underline this change, the Lord again appoints him "sentinel for the house of Israel". In the face of the people's near despair – some are claiming that "The way of the Lord is not just" – and their fear that their fate is already sealed, the principle of personal responsibility (cf. chapter 18) is repeated. Sinners can repent; what matters is not past behaviour but present intent. An assurance is given that the Lord always longs to forgive.

One issue faces Ezekiel immediately: those in Jerusalem who have survived the Babylonian onslaught are claiming that, as the true descendants of Abraham, they, not those in exile, are entitled to the land. Ezekiel's reply is that those in Jerusalem are committing the very sins that led to disaster in the first place. "The implication… is that the Lord's fresh start will be made with the exiles, not with those who remain in the land of Judah. The judgement therefore is an implicit word of hope for the people in exile."[12] There is also a word of hope for the prophet: though people flock to him in numbers as though to an entertainer, "a singer of love songs", without any intention of responding, the Lord promises that Ezekiel's predictions will be borne out and then "they shall know that a prophet has been among them" (33:1-33).

---

11 The dating of the messenger's arrival suggests the journey took him seventeen months, but, as scholars point out, a slight emendation of the Hebrew would make his journey a much more reasonable five months!

12 L. Boadt CSP, "Ezekiel", in R.E. Brown, J.A. Fitzmyer and R.E Murphy (eds), *The New Jerome Biblical Commentary* (London: G. Chapman, 1989), p. 322.

False shepherds and true shepherd

Ezekiel has strong words of condemnation for "the shepherds" who have failed in their pastoral responsibilities. Far from promoting the welfare of the people, they have taken advantage of them, showing no concern for the weak and the sick, and allowing those in their charge to be exiled and "scattered over all the face of the earth". Now the Lord warns that he will come to punish them and rescue the sheep. More than that, he will be their shepherd, seeking out the scattered flock, bringing them back to their own land where they will dwell in good pastures beside flowing watercourses. But there is judgement not only for venal shepherds but also for powerful sheep that abuse weak ones by fouling the water, butting and scattering "the lean sheep" out of the way. God promises to raise up a human shepherd, the shepherd-king David – not of course the David who died centuries before, but one of his line: a Davidic prince will be their king. The rest of the chapter speaks of the "covenant of peace" God will make and how the people will enjoy rich blessings, security and freedom from oppression. And the Lord will say: "You are my sheep, the sheep of my pasture and I am your God" (34:1-31).

Disaster for Edom and restoration for exiles

Once again Edom – here addressed as Mount Seir – is condemned by Ezekiel, as he sets his face firmly against it. Because Edomites attempted to take over "these two countries", Israel and Judah, "at the time of their final punishment", the Lord threatens them with destruction, but with the threats comes a four-times repeated assertion that then Edom will "know… the Lord". The fate of Edom serves as a foil to the restoration promised to the exiles. As Mount Seir was commanded to hear the word of the Lord, so the "mountains of Israel" are given a similar command, but this time it is a word not of condemnation but of hope. Despite devastation, the land will be renewed and will flourish in preparation for the homecoming exiles and the rebuilding of cities. The Lord will bring back "my people Israel"; the land will be their inheritance and no longer will they fear the mockery or depredations of other nations. Restoration of the land will be accompanied by renewal of the people. In the past they brought shame on God's name and on themselves, so that other nations mockingly said: "These are the people of the Lord, and yet they had to go out of his land." Even in exile they continued to profane God's name by their idolatrous behaviour. So now, "for the sake of my holy name", they will be gathered from all the countries and brought home. God will cleanse them from their idols with a sprinkling of "clean water"; then renew them internally by giving them "a new spirit" and "a new heart"; and, after removing their "heart of stone", will transplant within them a "heart of flesh", responsive to the divine spirit, so that at last, thanks to the Lord's initiative, they will be empowered to follow his laws and ordinances. Then, "you shall be my people, and I will be your God". They will enjoy plentiful crops, see places of desolation become "like the garden of Eden", regret their evil ways and understand that what has happened is a vindication of the Lord (35:1 – 36:38).

Third great vision: "Dem bones, dem dry bones"

The third great vision begins, like the previous ones, with the words: "The hand of the Lord came upon me." Ezekiel is "set... down in the middle of a valley", presumably where the first vision occurred, but this time it is "full of bones". They are an apt symbol of a devastated nation and are identified as "the whole house of Israel", a nation that openly declares: "our hope is lost". As Ezekiel wanders through the desolate scene, he is asked by the Lord, "Can these bones live?" Hesitantly, he replies: "O Lord God, you know." He is told to "prophesy to these bones", proclaiming in God's name that sinews and flesh, skin and breath will come to them. There's the rattling sound of bone upon bone and the sight of bones being clad with sinews and flesh and skin, but as yet no breath is in them. At a second divine command, Ezekiel summons the breath from all four winds. It enters them and at once an army of living bodies stands in the valley. The Lord God explains that he is going to open the graves of his people, enable them to rise and lead them back "to the land of Israel". Then, filled with "my spirit" (*ruach*), they will recognise him as Lord.

If the first image of restoration is new life breathed into the as-good-as-dead exiles, the second, no less striking, is the reunification of Israel. "The prospect of an eventual union between the northern tribes and Judah must have seemed as unrealistic in Ezekiel's day as the unification of the churches will appear to most contemporary Christians."[13] But that is what the prophet promises, illustrating the message by joining together two pieces of wood as though making them a single stick; on one is written the name of Judah (and its allies), on the other the name of Joseph (that is, the northern tribes). He explains that the Lord will gather all the exiled tribes, bring them back to their own land and make them "one nation"; "never again shall they be divided into two kingdoms", and "one king shall be king over them all" – "my servant David" (cf. chapter 34). An "everlasting covenant" will be struck and a Temple will be established as "my dwelling place... among them for evermore" (37:1-28).

Gog and Magog

The restoration of Israel is announced through stories that are strange, even by the standards of Ezekiel. They are apocalyptic in style, a type of writing meant to encourage God's people in difficult times and incorporating

---

[13] Blenkinsopp, *Ezekiel*, p. 174.

visions and strange imagery. The Lord is going to punish "Gog, of the land of Magog", who is "chief prince of Meshech and Tubal" and has many allies. He and his confederates will invade Israel when the risk of war seems so remote that cities have no defensive walls, bars or gates. Gog and Magog are mythical, like characters and places in a fairy story. Gog symbolises all the nations that threaten Israel, but in the end it will be the Lord's greatness and holiness that will triumph. There will be upheavals in land, sea and air; mountains, cliffs and walls will tumble; sword and pestilence will visit Gog and his cohorts; and from the heavens will come torrential rain, fire and brimstone. The bodies of Gog and his troops will be food for bird and beast; and the burning of their weapons will provide so much fuel that Israel will have no need to cut down trees for seven years. The remains of the fallen will be buried in a location as fictitious as Gog and Magog. The cleansing of the land will be followed by a celebratory meal in which the enemy is the feast, and the birds and beasts the guests! Ezekiel has a message of hope: the house of Israel "shall know that I am the Lord their God" and nations will know that Israel's exile was due to their unfaithfulness.

But when the Lord restores their fortunes "they shall forget their shame", or, according to another reading, they "shall not forget", in the sense that they will learn from the past and so will live securely "with no one to make them afraid... and I [the Lord] will never again hide my face from them" (38:1 – 39:29).

Fourth great vision: the Lord's return to the restored city

This "extended vision is an integral conclusion to the book as a whole... a theological symbol of the ideal relationship of Israel to Yahweh for the future".[14]

New Temple

In "the twenty-fifth year of our exile" Ezekiel is taken to a "very high mountain" overlooking Jerusalem and an angelic (?) figure, armed with "cord and a measuring reed", leads him round a new Temple, urging him to tell his compatriots all he sees and hears. A huge wall, over ten feet high and wide, surrounds the Temple area. On three sides are gateways that stand at the top of seven steps and lead to a huge outer court with a surrounding pavement and numerous chambers to meet the needs of worshippers. (A building along the western wall prevents access from that direction.) Gates on the inner walls correspond to those on the outer walls; they are approached by eight steps and open onto the inner courtyard reserved for the priests.

---

[14] Boadt, "Ezekiel", p. 326 §91.

As flights of steps emphasise the increasing level of holiness as one approaches God's house, so different degrees of spatial closeness to the most sacred area of the Temple – first the vestibule, then the sanctuary or nave, and finally the Holy of Holies – serve the same purpose.[15] Only the High Priest is allowed to enter the "most holy place", and he only on the Day of Atonement (Yom Kippur). The Temple has high windows, is ornamented with woodcarvings, and "something resembling an altar of wood" stands before "the holy place". On leaving the building, Ezekiel's companion leads him back to the outer court and indicates other buildings that serve the priests as sacristies. Finally, he measures the four exterior walls. The purpose of all the detailed measuring is stated: "to make a separation between the holy and the common" (40:1 – 42:20).

Return of the "glory"

Ezekiel is taken to the eastern gate to witness a climactic vision: "the glory of the God of Israel", which he had seen leaving the Temple and moving towards the east, he now sees returning to the restored Temple, and falls down in worship. In the inner court the Lord assures him that "this is the place of my throne… where I will reside among the people of Israel for ever". In the past Temple and royal palace formed one complex so that a wicked king, like Manasseh, could turn the Temple into a private chapel for Baal worship. That will not happen again: the Temple is to stand completely apart. Ezekiel is to teach the people the laws governing the Temple, and give detailed instructions about the altar of burnt offering, which only after a seven-day ceremony of consecration will be ready for use. Finally, returning to the east wall of the outer court, the prophet sees that the gate is closed and is told it must remain so, for it is via this gate that God re-entered the Temple.

Back in the inner court, Ezekiel prostrates himself as another vision of "the glory of the Lord" fills the Temple. He is told that the people, a "rebellious house", are to follow meticulously the Temple regulations and that the Levites, who abetted them in wrongdoing, are to serve but in more menial Temple ministries. However, the sons of Zadok, who remained faithful, are to be the sacrificial priests, wearing linen garments for worship, keeping their hair trimmed, drinking no wine before entering the inner court and marrying only a virgin or the widow of another priest. Thus, by example as by word, "they shall teach my people the difference between the holy and the common… the unclean and the clean". Though entitled to a portion of the sacrifices, they are to own no land, for "I [the Lord] am their inheritance" (43:1 – 44:31).

---

[15] The three areas are, respectively, thirty-five by twenty-one feet, thirty-five by seventy feet and thirty-five feet square.

The territory "set aside for the Lord" is to be divided into three strips: the northern one for the Levites and the middle one, with the Temple at its centre and an open space around it, for the priests. These two strips constitute "a holy district", so that "the entire temple is now the holy of holies… a kind of temple within the greater temple of the sacred enclosure".[16] The third strip, half the size of the others, is for "the whole house of Israel". Finally, "the prince" has territory to the west of the sacred enclosure and is to rule with justice, ensuring the use of just weights and measures. This leads logically to rules about appropriate contributions, by weight and measure, for the upkeep of the prince and his court.

On New Year's Day (in March in Ezekiel's day) the Temple is to be purified, following a rite similar to that for the dedication of the altar. There are detailed regulations about the contributions the prince is to make to the seven-day feasts of Passover and Tabernacles, as well as in celebrations for the new moon and the sabbath. On the latter days, and on other special occasions, the inner east gate is opened and the prince allowed to approach, acting like a mediator between priests (in the inner court) and people (beyond the outer gate) and presenting sacrificial gifts to the clergy. Additional instructions concern the entrances and exits of the Temple by the prince and "the people of the land", the amount of oil and grain to accompany ritual sacrifices and the limitations placed upon the prince in the disposition of his estates. Finally, the angelic guide leads Ezekiel on a further tour to ensure that regulations about the purity of the Temple are being observed (45:1 – 46:24).

Wondrous stream

An immediate result of the Lord's return to his Temple is the appearance of a stream, initially no more than a trickle of water coming from under the main eastern gate. But after travelling round the perimeter wall, Ezekiel and his companion see the stream gushing forth from the Temple towards the east. Four times, at thousand-cubit intervals, they take soundings and find the water is first ankle-deep, then knee-deep, then "up to the waist", and finally "a river that could not be crossed". The waters flow to the Dead Sea, turning its stagnant salt water into clean fresh water where fish abound; and on each side of the river are "a great many trees", each bearing "fresh fruit every month" and leaves with healing qualities. This picture of an arid land transformed into a paradise is, like the vision of the dry bones, an arresting image of the renewal the Lord will accomplish for his people: they, a renewed people, will return to a renewed land, with a renewed Temple, and there God will dwell with them (47:1-12).

---

[16] Blenkinsopp, *Ezekiel*, p. 223.

The first Exodus had ended with a division of land among the twelve tribes; so too will the exodus-return of the exiles. After a delineation of the country's boundaries, the land is apportioned in equal strips, running from east to west, to each of the tribes. The territory of seven tribes is to the north of the sacred area set apart for the Temple personnel and the prince, and the territory of the other five to the south. The book ends with a final return to the city, whose twelve gateways bear the names of the twelve tribes. This is Israel's city, but its name – "The Lord is There" – makes clear it is above all the city of the Lord (47:13 – 48:35).

After the exile, the reality may have fallen far short of Ezekiel's vision, but the words and imagery of the prophet have had a powerful influence on Jewish and Christian thought. The good shepherd promised by Ezekiel (chapter 34) takes flesh in Jesus, who has compassion for the crowd that are "like sheep without a shepherd" (Mark 6:34), who tells the parable of the lost sheep (Matthew 18:12-14) and who calls himself the Good Shepherd (John 10:11). A new "holy temple" appears with Christ as its "cornerstone" (Ephesians 2:20-22) and his followers as its "living stones" (1 Peter 2:5). From the side of Jesus, the "holy temple", springs the "living water" of the Holy Spirit (John 7:37-38), as well as the water and blood (John 19:34), symbolising the sacraments. Jesus is Immanuel, "a name which means, 'God is with us'" (Matthew 1:23-24), and he is here in our midst "to the end of the age" (Matthew 28:20). Finally, Ezekiel's contribution to apocalyptic writing comes to fruition in the book of the Apocalypse. There, many of the prophet's images reappear: the chariot of God, Gog and Magog, the angelic guide with a measuring rod and the holy city, the heavenly Jerusalem, where "the wall of the city has twelve foundations, and on them are the twelve names of the twelve apostles of the Lamb" (Apocalypse 21:14).

9 Isaiah II
– heralding a new exodus

The author of the second part of Isaiah is unknown. There is the delightful suggestion that he was like one of the shadowy figures from the resistance movement during World War II who circulated secret tracts to encourage compatriots but remained nameless for fear of reprisals. Whatever the reason for his anonymity, Isaiah II has written as magnificently as any prophet; his work is "a great artistic achievement, and, theologically... unsurpassed".[1] It dates probably from the late 550s BC, when the emergence of Cyrus presaged the fall of Babylon. "Isaiah II" (or "Deutero-Isaiah") suggests indebtedness to Isaiah of Jerusalem, and in fact there are many links between them; for example, "Holy One of Israel", so typical of Isaiah I, appears no fewer than eleven times in the sixteen chapters of Isaiah II.

But there are also significant differences. Chapter 40 presupposes a historical situation quite different from that of the previous thirty-nine chapters: the exile is soon to end; the dateline has moved from mid eighth to late sixth century; the addressees are not wealthy citizens of Jerusalem but poor, despairing exiles in Babylon. There are theological differences too: the threats of earlier chapters now give way to such a tone of comfort and hope that Isaiah II has been called "the Book of Consolation". Central to it is the idea of a new exodus, which will give God's people a fresh opportunity to be faithful, leaving idol worship behind for ever.[2] In contrast to the idols, the Lord is mighty Creator, Redeemer, and transcendently Holy One; God's uniqueness may be implicit in other prophets – in Isaiah II it is stated explicitly and often.

Embedded in the book are the four "Servant Songs", which are "certainly an integral part of [the prophet's] message".[3] But who is the servant? An individual such as Moses or Jeremiah or even Isaiah II himself? Or does he represent the exiles, regularly referred to as "the servant" of the Lord? In any event, by the beginning of the Christian era the Songs were read by some Jews in a messianic sense; and in the Gospels Jesus is identified as the perfect Suffering Servant (Matthew 12:17-21; Mark 10:45).

"Comfort, O comfort, my people"

The opening words, with the double command typical of Isaiah II, ring out like a trumpet call. Addressed to the heavenly court, they promise

---

[1] J.M. Ward, *Thus Says the Lord* (Nashville: Abingdon Press, 1991), p. 80.
[2] Ward, *Thus Says the Lord*, p. 81.
[3] J. Drane, *Introducing the Old Testament* (Oxford: Lion, 2000), p. 192.

"tender" assurance to Jerusalem (that is, the exiles), for she is to receive no further punishment. God will lead a new exodus, this time from Babylon. Everything possible must be done to facilitate "the way of the Lord": crooked paths straightened out, mountains pulled down and "uneven ground" made "level" (words spoken by John the Baptist in the Gospels). And "the glory of the Lord" will be manifested to "all people".

The call to prophesy which follows is the only personal glimpse we have of Isaiah II. The command "Cry out!" is followed by a hesitant query: "What shall I cry?" The hesitancy arises from the abiding fear of the exiles that they have no future, that like other nations they are transient, with no more hold on existence than "the grass [that] withers" and "the flower [that] fades". But a pledge is given that though grass and flower may have no future, "the word of our God will stand for ever". On this assurance prophet and people can depend.

The initial message is repeated and "Zion" commanded to bring to all the cities of Judah the "good tidings": "Here is your God!" God comes with "might" and yet cares for the people as a shepherd cares for his flock: gathering them, feeding them, carrying the weak ones ("the lambs") "in his bosom". This description of the Saviour's closeness and gentleness is followed by a splendid portrayal of his might, so that within a single chapter we have a brilliant word-picture of both the intimacy and the transcendence of God. The section begins with a series of rhetorical questions, characteristic of Deutero-Isaiah, each inviting the answer: "No one, but our God." Thus, only our God can gather in cupped hands the waters of sea and ocean, or measure the vast expanse of the heavens with the span of a hand, or weigh the hills and mountains on a scale. Only our God is without need of a counsellor. To our God "even the nations are like a drop from a bucket", as insubstantial as dust on the scales. Not even Lebanon, renowned for its huge cedars, could provide "fuel enough" for our great God, or "animals enough" for a worthy sacrifice in his honour.

A further rhetorical question: "To whom then will you liken God?" And the answer is obvious: nothing and no one is comparable with "the Holy One" of Israel, least of all the idols. An idol is of human devising, and the "artisan" who sets it up has to ensure it "will not topple" to the ground! Again, a question: "Have you not heard" that our God, who transforms chaos into order, "created" the universe? ("To create" [bara'] always has God as its subject: creation is uniquely God's work.) With almighty power God "brings princes to naught" and the stars, which feature prominently in Babylonian worship, are God's handiwork, created effortlessly by a word.

Why, then, do the people lose heart? Haven't they heard that the Lord is "everlasting", "does not faint or grow weary", "gives power to the faint, and strengthens the powerless"? The exiles are to take heart. "Those who wait for the Lord" will be revitalised; they will mount upon buffeting winds as though with the wings of an eagle, they will "run and not be weary", "walk and not faint" (40:1-31).

Israel's liberator

Summoned to a trial, the nations are asked to say who stirred up Cyrus of Persia, conqueror of kings and nations, including Babylon. Faced with silence, the Lord responds: "I, the Lord", who am first and last. The Gentiles have to encourage each other because their idols are incapable of offering encouragement, but "you, Israel, my servant" and "my friend", have no need to fear: "I will uphold you with my victorious right hand." In the misery of exile they may feel as insignificant as a "worm", but they are assured, for the third time: "I will help you." Their "Redeemer" is "the Holy One of Israel". (A "redeemer" [go'el] was the nearest blood relative; he had sacred duties to his next of kin in misfortune [for example to avenge bloodshed, and raise up children to his brother's childless widow]. The Lord is the Redeemer of Israel because of a family connection established by the "marriage bond" of the covenant.) His redeeming work will transform wasteland into springs of water for those who are thirsty, so that it "ceases to be the pitiless, insurmountable barrier between the exiles and their homeland. It becomes a highway."[4] Israel's homecoming will mirror what happened at the Exodus. Even the pagans will "understand, that the hand of the Lord has done this".

In a second trial speech God challenges the gods of Babylon to show that they foretold "what is to happen" or are able to foretell "what is to come hereafter". The obvious conclusion from their silence is that their claims, like their deeds, "are nothing". In fact it was the Lord who "stirred up one from the north [Cyrus]" and declared in advance what would happen. And so comes the verdict: "they [the pagan gods] are all a delusion" and "their images are empty wind" (41:1-29).

First Servant Song – 42:1-9 (or 1-4 or 1-7)

God introduces the servant as one "whom I uphold, my chosen, in whom my soul delights". Filled with "my spirit", he will "bring forth justice to the nations" and establish it "in the earth"; but he will do so with gentleness and respect for others, not breaking the "bruised reed" or extinguishing the "dimly burning wick". The servant will fulfil his duty without growing

---

[4] C. Westermann, *Isaiah 40–66* (Philadelphia: Westminster Press, 1969), p. 80.

faint or being crushed by the opposition he will face. People in distant lands are waiting for what he has to say. The Lord says, "I have called you" (presumably, the servant), assures him that he has taken him "by the hand" and raised him "as a covenant to the people, a light to the nations"; he is to bring sight to the blind and release to captives. The Lord announces that his name is unique and that praise is due to him alone, not to the idols. He speaks of the "new things" that he has done, a reference to the forthcoming return from exile, glimpsed as a present reality. (The Song becomes richly significant when applied to Jesus, as in Mark 1:11 [his baptism], Matthew 12:20 [his gentleness] and Matthew 17:5 [his transfiguration].)

God's power and majesty

In response the prophet calls for a "new song" to be sung to the God of Israel, opening with words used in Psalms 96 and 98. Praise should be raised to the ends of the earth, in desert villages where the nomadic Kedarites live and in "Sela" (Petra), renowned capital of Edom. Praise is due to the Lord as a mighty warrior who seemed deaf to the pleas of the exiles, but now "shows himself mighty against his foes". For a time he "held [his] peace", but now he is like a woman in travail – neither still nor silent! Desert will become fertile land for the sake of his people, and fertile land a desert for the sake of his enemies, the idolaters, who will be "utterly put to shame". His own people are "deaf": in the misery of exile, they felt that there was no future for them and that God had abandoned them. They, God's "servant" and "dedicated one", have been not only deaf but blind too, failing to learn lessons from God's mighty deeds of the past or appreciate that present disasters are punishment from the God "in whose ways they would not walk". Once the people acknowledge that the present plight is of their own making, the Lord, who "created" and "formed" them, responds in words warm with promise: "Do not fear, for I have redeemed you"; he will be with them in their exodus journey from exile because "you are mine". He, "the Holy One", the Lord of creation and of history, proclaims that they are more "precious in my sight" than mighty nations, such as Egypt. Thus, "a tiny miserable and insignificant band of uprooted men and women are assured that they... are the people to whom God has turned in love; they, just as they are, are dear and precious in his sight... and if Israel hearkens to... the assurance of salvation... nothing can be too miraculous in the way her redemption is brought about",[5] even if they should pass through water or flames of fire. They are told, "Do not fear", and assured that wherever they may be – north, south, east or west – they will be called back home.

---

[5] Westermann, *Isaiah 40–66*, p. 118.

Another trial scene between God and the gods of the nations opens up; again the issue is their claim to divinity, but this time the Lord's witnesses are the people of Israel, even though they often behaved as though blind and deaf. The question put to the "gods" is: which of them ever foretold the future? Without waiting for a reply, the Lord declares that there never was a god before him, nor will there be after him. This is a theological statement that Israel's God is the only God; there is no other. As the "Redeemer", the Lord will visit Babylon, break down its bars and set prisoners free. He is the "Holy One" who created Israel by making a pathway for them through the Sea of Reeds and luring the Egyptians to a watery grave. But they are urged not to "remember the former things" as though they were simply past, but rather to see that even now their Liberator is launching "a new thing" – a repeat performance, as we might say, involving the making of a way for his people through the wilderness, where he will "give water" to transform desert and provide drink for beasts and people. And "the people whom I formed for myself" will "declare my praise".

Then the Lord brings a charge against them: in their worship they have acted hypocritically. They have wearied him; instead of being his servants, they have tried to make him their servant. Though from the beginning (the time of "your first ancestor") Israel "sinned" and so was "delivered… to utter destruction", yet he declares that "for my own sake… I will not remember your sins". On the contrary, the comforting cry "Do not fear" is repeated, followed by the promise of salvation to "Jacob my servant, Israel whom I have chosen" and formed in the womb. As the Lord's child, Israel is affectionately called *yeshurun* ("darling"[6]). Fresh streams of water will be poured over "dry" and "thirsty" Israel. The new era will lead to further blessings upon "your descendants": their growth and prosperity will, on the one hand, be like that of luxuriant trees beside streams, and on the other will result in an ever-increasing number of Gentiles who worship the Lord. He is "King of Israel", "Redeemer", "Lord of hosts", "first and… last"; as his people can bear witness, only he has been a true "rock" of refuge for them (42:10 – 44:8).

Omnipotence v. impotence

A biting satire on the makers of idols begins with the statement that "All who make idols are nothing" (*tohu*), that idol devotees ("witnesses") never derive any good from them, and that makers and worshippers alike "shall all be put to shame". Then comes a mocking description of how the idols are made: once the material is procured it has to be decided whether to use the

---

[6] C. Stuhlmueller CP, "Deutero-Isaiah and Trito-Isaiah", in R.E. Brown, J.A. Fitzmyer and R.E. Murphy (eds), *The New Jerome Biblical Commentary* (London: G. Chapman, 1989), p. 336.

wood for a fire to cook a meal or to turn it into an idol, and, if the latter, then the maker falls down before it, crying, "Save me, for you are my god!" How foolish can you be! In striking contrast Israel is fashioned to the glory of God, and its sins have been "swept away... like mist". All creation – heavens and depths of earth, mountains and forests – are invited to sing in praise of the Lord's redeeming work.

Unlike the useless idols, the Lord, as creator of all things and Lord of history, redeems his people: Jerusalem "shall be rebuilt", even though it will be accomplished with the aid of Cyrus. "He is my shepherd," says the Lord, "and he shall carry out all my purpose." The Lord invests him as king (cf. Psalms 2 and 110), as his "anointed", a title never before bestowed on a non-Israelite; he grasps him by his right hand[7] and calls him by name, thereby confirming his royal status; and finally gives him a solemn message: he will be successful in his conquest, for "I will go before you." So people from east to west will recognise that "I am the Lord, and there is no other." All this "though you [Cyrus] do not know me", all this "for the sake of... Israel my chosen". The commissioning of Cyrus ends with a brief hymn begging the Lord to send down his abundant blessings like rain and raise up salvation like a crop from the earth.[8]

Israelites who question the Lord for using Cyrus as his instrument and speaking of him as his "anointed" are reproached. They are as foolish as a clay pot criticising the potter or a child its parent. As for those who suggest the Lord is responsible for their sufferings, the Holy One retorts that he raised up Cyrus precisely so that he might "set my exiles free". Peoples from the ends of the earth will be brought to Jerusalem, will bring gifts to the Temple, confessing that there is no god but the Lord. Reflecting on the Lord's use of human instruments such as Cyrus, the prophet declares: "Truly, you are a God who hides himself"; nonetheless, you are the "Saviour" of your people, in contrast to the idol-makers who will all be "put to shame".

The Lord created the world for all the nations, but for his own people he is no "hidden God"; as he brought order out of chaos, so he will transform their exile by a new creation. In the meantime the "survivors of the nations", presumably Babylonians who escaped when their city fell, are summoned to appear and asked: who foretold long ago the disaster that has befallen them? "Was it not I, the Lord?" But, far from rejoicing in their defeat, the Lord offers a wonderful invitation: "Turn to me and be saved." He proclaims that

---

[7] At their coronation Babylonian kings grasped the right hand of their national god, Marduk. See Stuhlmueller, "Deutero-Isaiah", p. 337.

[8] Jerome's translation of the "just one" (for "justice") and the "saviour" (for "salvation") made verse 8 an appropriate Advent cry and is the first line of the Latin Advent hymn *Rorate caeli desuper*.

"every knee" is called to bow before him, recognising that he alone is Lord (cf. Philippians 2:10, where every knee will bow to the risen Lord).

In the flight from Babylon, Bel and Nebo, the national gods, unable to save even themselves, will be loaded upon beasts of burden. Israel is urged to remember how, in striking contrast, the Lord has borne "all the remnant of the house of Israel" from the day of their birth and will continue to do so into their old age. What folly, then, to treat the Lord and the idols "as though we were alike". They are purchased from the goldsmith and their owners then place them in their places where they stand, motionless and deaf to every prayer. Those who resort to idols are urged to "remember the former things", all that the Lord has done for them in the past; in particular how he foretold all that has happened and is now effecting the salvation promised by summoning "a bird of prey from the east" (Cyrus), a man "from a far country"; and so "I will put salvation in Zion" (44:9 – 46:13).

Fall of Babylon

Having mocked Babylon's gods, the prophet now mocks Babylon herself in a lament in which "the prophet's virtuosity is displayed".[9] She is likened to a young girl, "tender and delicate" in her courtly elegance and luxury, who is ordered to come down from her throne and "sit in the dust", like a servant girl busy with menial tasks; her fine clothes stripped off, she will be publicly humiliated. All this is the work of "Our Redeemer – the Lord of hosts… the Holy One of Israel". The prophet's audacity is remarkable: he is describing how "the vanquished God of a petty, vanquished nation takes vengeance on the mighty colossus of Babylon".[10] The reason for Babylon's disaster is twofold: first, because when Israel was given "into your hand", "you showed them no mercy"; second, because Babylon has displayed such arrogance, imagining "I shall be mistress for ever" and even making the claim that the Lord alone can make – "I am, and there is no one besides me." Research has revealed the considerable intellectual achievements of the Babylonian empire, but Isaiah II suggests that it was this "wisdom and… knowledge" that gave the people a false sense of security and so led to their downfall. Nothing can save them now, certainly not the astrologers who play such an important part in their lives (47:1-15).

The people are commanded to "hear". Whether from the northern tribes or the southern, they are descendants of the one patriarch, Jacob; they worship one God, belong to "the holy city" and "lean [in trust] on the God of Israel". They know from their history that the Lord fulfils what he has promised,

---

[9] Westermann, *Isaiah 40–66*, p. 190.
[10] Westermann, *Isaiah 40–66*, p. 191.

even if it does not happen immediately and in the end takes them by surprise. But now they are to hear "new things" – not simply the fall of Babylon but also news of their return from exile. The Lord will do this not because they deserve it but for his own glory. (Several textual difficulties, and also harsh comments about Israel out of tune with the immediate context, suggest that parts of this chapter are additions from an unknown source.)

Israel is to "listen to me", the One who is "the first, and... the last", who is creator of heaven and earth so that at his word "they [his creation] stand at attention". "The Lord loves him" (Cyrus) who is to "perform [the Lord's] purpose on Babylon". The Lord has always had his people's interests at heart, always wanted to lead them "in the way [they] should go". How different things might have been, had they been obedient!

The prophet speaks explicitly about the "new thing" the Lord will do: God's people will "Go out from Babylon". There will be shouts of joy; to the ends of the earth they will hear that "The Lord has redeemed his servant Jacob!" Mindful of how the people were cared for during the Exodus, the exiles can be confident that God will look after them on their journey home through the desert. However, "the wicked" will not experience "peace" (*shalom*) (48:1-22).

Second Servant Song – 49:1-6

The servant tells how, like Jeremiah, he was called from the womb and given a mission centred upon the word, so that his mouth is "like a sharp sword", penetrating deeply; he is like "a polished arrow", able to reach distant places, though lying hidden "in [the Lord's] quiver" till the appropriate time. His Master will be glorified in him, and yet, like Jeremiah and many another prophet, he is filled with despondency, fearing that his work has been in vain. The Lord insists that the servant's commission, like Jeremiah's, goes beyond Israel: it is to be "a light to the nations", so that salvation is brought "to the end of the earth".

Joyful homecoming

"The Lord, the Redeemer of Israel and his Holy One", declares that Israel, though "despised" and made "the slave of rulers", will be restored. Then kings and princes of the nations will be astonished and will come to acknowledge the Lord's sovereignty. "In a time of favour", the Lord has answered the prayers of his people; "on a day of salvation", he has come to their help. The prisoners are to "Come out" of the "darkness" of captivity. God, the Good Shepherd, will lead a new exodus journey for all the exiles; they will know neither hunger nor thirst, neither biting wind nor burning sun. He has indeed "comforted his people", as promised in the opening words of Isaiah II. The whole of creation participates in a chorus of praise.

Three questions raised by the people lead to a deeper understanding of what God is doing for them. The first expresses what the exiles must often have thought – why had the Lord forgotten them? The response ranks among the most glorious passages in the Bible: "Can a woman forget her nursing child, or show no compassion for the child of her womb? Even these may forget, yet I will not forget you." God's love surpasses even that of a mother for her child. The people of God are "inscribed… on the palms of my hands", never to be shaken off, never forgotten. The exiles, streaming back from every land, will be like a bride's ornament, though not so much a token of beauty as a sign that Israel has regained her reputation before the nations. Indeed, so great will be the number of returning exiles that the land will seem too small to hold them. The second question asks: where have all these children come from, since "I [Israel] was bereaved and barren, exiled and put away"? This time the response takes the form of a promise that the Lord will raise his hand, a sign he is entering into battle with their enemies; and so Israel's sons and daughters will be restored. Israel can be assured that "those who wait for me shall not be put to shame". The final complaint is that the people of Israel find themselves the "prey" of a mighty power: how can they "be rescued"? The Lord's answer is that he will tear the prey away from the "mighty"; he will save Israel's children. A traditional description of a defeated nation is added, including the horrific prospect of "oppressors" resorting to cannibalism. But Isaiah II's real concern is with the freeing of God's people and what will result from it: not only Israel but "all flesh" will know who has been at work – "the Lord, your Saviour and your Redeemer, the Mighty One of Jacob" (49:7-26).

The separation of the Lord from his spouse, Israel, in the exile was punishment for her infidelity, but the separation was never meant to be absolute. Let no one say the Lord's hand is "shortened, that it cannot redeem", for he has power over all creation (50:1-3).

Third Servant Song – 50:4-9

The servant hears like one who is taught and speaks like one who teaches; he is a disciple and "morning by morning" the Lord opens his ear and gives him a message so that he may "sustain the weary with a word" of comfort. He stands firm in his task, setting his "face like flint", despite suffering grievously at the hands of his enemies; he has not resisted those who struck his back, pulled his beard and insulted him with spittle. He asserts: "I shall not be put to shame… the Lord God… helps me."

Trust in the Lord

The prophet encourages the faithful with a reminder of what the Lord did for Abraham, "the rock from which you were hewn", and Sarah "who bore you". Though past the age of childbearing, they became the parents of many people. By a similar creative act, the Lord will transform the position of Zion, making her into a new Eden, alive with "joy and gladness", "thanksgiving and the voice of song". Then, picking up a theme of the second Servant Song about the universality of his mission, the prophet reminds the people that the Lord's "teaching", "light" and "salvation" are already on the way to the nations. Though "the heavens will vanish like smoke" and "the earth… wear out like a garment", God's salvation will endure for ever.

There is a triple cry of "Awake, awake". The first, addressed to the "arm of the Lord", begs God to repeat the wonderful deeds of old. A Middle Eastern myth saw creation as the victory of a creator god over "Rahab", a sea monster. Isaiah II uses the myth as a metaphor for the way God the Creator brought order out of a primordial watery chaos, but also for the way God the Redeemer "dried up the sea" at the Exodus. Those who escaped from Egypt were filled with joy, and those ransomed from Babylon will "come to Zion with singing… and sorrow and sighing shall flee away". While reproving them for being afraid of their oppressor, "a mere mortal", and forgetting that he is their Creator, the Lord also gives the assurance that the "oppressed shall speedily be released".

The second appeal is to Jerusalem: "Rouse yourself, rouse yourself!" In exile she was prostrate with grief, experienced "devastation and destruction, famine and sword" and drank deeply of "the bowl of [the Lord's] wrath"; but now he will take the cup away from his people and "put it into the hand of your tormentors", who literally walked over them – a common humiliation for prisoners. The final appeal, again addressed to Jerusalem, is that she must "Put on [her] beautiful garments" as for a festival, now that she has risen "from the dust" and loosened the bonds of captivity. No longer will the "unclean" dwell there. If she was "sold for nothing" to the Babylonians, now she is to be "redeemed without money", thanks to God's graciousness. Those released from Egypt were later oppressed by the Assyrians, just as now the people are oppressed by the Babylonians. But the Lord has no intention of staying with them in a place where his name is "despised"; he will bring them home; and then "they shall know that it is I" who have been at work (50:10 – 52:6).

Messenger with good news

And now a messenger arrives; his feet are "beautiful" because they bear one who brings "good news" of the Lord's triumph and "announces peace" and "salvation" for the people. No longer is it is an earthly ruler, but "Your God [who] reigns" in Jerusalem, and is "celebrated in the 'psalms of the reign of Yahweh'".[11] He "has bared his holy arm before the eyes of all the nations"; he has returned in triumphal procession to Jerusalem and there been hailed as King. To the voice of the messenger are added those of the "sentinels" guarding the city walls, who actually "see the return of the Lord". Finally, the chorus is enlarged by the joyful singing of the "ruins of Jerusalem", that is, "the suffering, bewildered and weary remnant of the nation in the exile".[12] The Lord has indeed "comforted his people". In this new exodus, "God will go before and after, like the pillars of fire and cloud", and the return will have "the character of a religious procession from the profane place of Babylon to the sacred area of Jerusalem".[13] Those who carry "the vessels of the Lord", once stolen by the Babylonians from the Temple but now returned by Cyrus, must purify themselves for their sacred task (52:7-12).

Fourth Servant Song – 52:13 – 53:12

The final Servant Song is the most extraordinary. It begins with the proclamation that "my servant shall prosper... shall be exalted and lifted up", but only after he has endured humiliations that reduce him to a semblance of humanity, so that many are appalled at his condition. And yet kings and nations will finally be astonished at his exaltation; they will witness something they could never have imagined. The servant came from humble stock, "was despised and rejected" by his own people, endured pains and sufferings that made him "a man of suffering [sorrows]", and was treated like an outcast. In a kind of parenthesis stands the amazing statement that in all this he bore "*our* infirmities", that "we" (without indication of who "we" are) thought he was "struck down by God", but in fact "he was wounded for *our* transgressions" and "by his bruises *we* are healed" (emphases added). We behaved like sheep, each going our own way, while "the Lord has laid on him the iniquity of us all".

The account of the servant's sufferings continues: if "we" behaved like sheep, he has been like "a lamb... led to the slaughter" and has borne all without opening his mouth. He was done to death, "cut off from the land of the

---

[11] *The New Jerusalem Bible*, ed. H. Wansbrough (London: Darton, Longman & Todd, 1985), p. 1273, note e. The psalms referred to are 47, 93, 96, 97, 98, 99, 145 and 146.
[12] Westermann, *Isaiah 40–66*, p. 251.
[13] J.J. Collins, *Isaiah: Collegeville Bible Commentary*, no. 13 (Collegeville, MN: Liturgical Press, 1986), p. 113.

living", laid in a tomb with criminals and evildoers,[14] and yet was completely innocent. Then, in line with the thought of the parenthesis above, the song reports that all "was the will of the Lord" and that "through him [the servant] the will of the Lord shall prosper". Incredibly, the "righteous one, my servant, shall make many righteous", his days will be prolonged, and, because "he poured out himself unto death" and "made intercession for the transgressors", he will be richly rewarded.

The identity of the servant may remain a mystery, but two points seem clear. First, the prophet's contemporaries must have known to whom it referred, in all probability the nation in its suffering and prophetic mission to the world. Second, the song has a deeper level of meaning, revealed by the saving death and resurrection of Jesus, which is why the fourth Servant Song is part of the Good Friday liturgy.

God's eternal care

A splendid hymn proclaims the transformation taking place in Zion: she, "the barren one", bereft of inhabitants, is to "burst into song", for she is to have many children. In a series of imperatives, she is told to "enlarge", "lengthen", "strengthen" her dwellings so as to house her enlarged family. She need not "fear" or "be discouraged" or feel "shame" – common experiences of a childless wife or a vanquished nation – because she is no longer alone: "your Maker is your husband" – a return to Hosea's daring metaphor – and "the Holy One of Israel is your Redeemer". Once "like a wife forsaken", she was "abandoned" but only briefly, and now "with everlasting love" God "will have compassion" on her. Just as the Lord swore to Noah, "the waters… would never again go over the earth", so now he swears he will not abandon Zion. Even though mountains depart, "my steadfast love shall not depart from you".

There is further reassurance for Zion, once "storm-tossed" like Noah in the flood, because she is to be raised in splendour. She will be adorned with precious metals, her "foundations [will] reflect the green and deep blue of the sky; the golden doors reflect the blazing fire of the sun",[15] as though the prophet had the heavenly Jerusalem in mind. Moreover, her "children shall be taught by the Lord… great shall be the prosperity" and she will be safe from all "oppression" and "terror"; no threatening word or weapon of war will harm her. Such will be "the heritage of the servants of the Lord and their vindication" (54:1-17).

---

14 The reading "his tomb with the rich" seems to contradict what has just been said ("his grave with the wicked"). A slight emendation of the Hebrew would give "his grave with the evildoer".
15 Stuhlmueller, "Deutero-Isaiah", p. 343.

The final chapter invites the poor who "have no money" to come and enjoy food and drink without payment. Beyond satisfying bodily hunger and thirst, after the privations of exile, the Lord promises still richer blessings to those who "Listen carefully to me" and "come to me". They will enjoy a fullness of life they have not known before, because the Lord will make "an everlasting covenant" with them and they will experience the "steadfast, sure love" promised to David; the promises made to the great king are to be realised in the whole nation. David's achievements were a witness to the nations that the Lord was supporting his people, and now Israel is to be God's witness among the nations. The prophet raises a cry, familiar from earlier prophets, "Seek the Lord while he may be found, call upon him while he is near." He is near now, even in the land of exile. And "the wicked" are to take the opportunity to return to him "that he may have mercy on them".

Then, in words that sum up the whole book, Isaiah II tells his people that they can rely on the Lord to accomplish all he has promised because "as the heavens are higher than the earth so are [the Lord's] ways higher than your ways and [his] thoughts than your thoughts". As certainly as rain and snow accomplish their purpose of watering the earth and making it fertile, so the Lord's words always achieve their purpose. When the Lord speaks, not least through his prophets, he never speaks in vain.

By way of epilogue to this chapter – in which "Almost every major theme within chapters 40–54 is blended into [a] glorious finale"[16] – comes the proclamation that the people will "go out in joy, and be led back [home] in peace". Nature itself will join in the rejoicing and anything likely to hinder progress (such as thorn or brier) will be replaced by trees of paradise ("the cypress" and "the myrtle"). All to God's glory (55:1-13).

This magnificent book is dear to Christians, especially because of its Servant Songs with their "surplus" of meaning that is revealed – as Philip explained in the Ethiopian's chariot (Acts 8:32-35) – in the life and teaching, death and resurrection of Jesus Christ. He came in order "to give his life as a ransom for [the] many" (Mark 10:45), and humbled himself even to death on the cross, and so was highly exalted so that "every tongue should confess that Jesus Christ is Lord, to the glory of God the Father" (Philippians 2:6-11). It is highly significant that the Servant Songs are allotted a place year by year in the Church's Holy Week liturgy.

---

[16] Stuhlmueller, "Deutero-Isaiah", p. 343.

Section three
After the Exile

The post-exilic prophets

During the dark days of Israel's exile, the Babylonian empire begins to crumble. In 556 BC the last of Babylon's kings comes to the throne. He antagonises many by his allegiance to the moon god, at the expense of the national god Marduk. And so when Cyrus and the Persian armies descend upon Babylon, many citizens welcome them, some of the soldiers desert, and the city falls without a blow being struck. The following year (538), Cyrus allows exiled Jews to return home and rebuild their city and Temple, and at the same time restores the sacred vessels that had been looted by the Babylonians. In fact, a minority of the exiles returns; the rest are content to stay in Babylon with the businesses and lands they have acquired, the new friends they have made and the families that are now established there.

It is ISAIAH III who in the early post-exilic period offers support to those who do return. They experience great difficulties: the city is in ruins, the fields for the most part are uncultivated and they face hostility from the Samaritans who claim the land for themselves. Later, another group of exiles returns, under the leadership of Zerubbabel (grandson of Jehoiachin, the last legitimate Davidic king in the people's eyes), and Joshua, a priest. However, it is not until 520 that, spurred on by HAGGAI and ZECHARIAH, serious efforts are made to complete the reconstruction of the new Temple, which is finally dedicated in 515.

Sometime after this, three other prophets challenge the people. ZECHARIAH II, responsible for the last six chapters of the book attributed to Zechariah, speaks of a future when Israel will enjoy God's triumph. Then, as religious fervour cools and religious leaders grow negligent, the prophet MALACHI calls for a spiritual renewal. JOEL also urges the people to turn back to God while there is still time; he is much concerned with "the day of the Lord" and promises an outpouring of the Holy Spirit. The story told by JONAH, with its emphasis on God's boundless love for all, stands as a rebuke to the exclusiveness displayed by many of the Jews. Nehemiah, appointed governor of Jerusalem in 445, and Ezra, a priest (the date of his mission to Jerusalem is uncertain), are largely responsible for the rebuilding of the Jewish community in the city and the restoration of strict religious practices.

About two centuries after Cyrus' rise to power, the Persian empire comes to an end with the emergence of the Greeks. In 333 Alexander begins his incredible conquest of the ancient world: though dead by the age of thirty-three, he is remarkably successful in spreading Greek culture and thought wherever his armies go. On his death, the empire is divided between his four generals. One of their successors, Antiochus IV Epiphanes, launches bitter persecution against the Jews; he strives to impose the Greek way of life on the whole land, banning under pain of death the practice of the Jewish faith, the rite of circumcision and sabbath observance; he builds a pagan Greek centre in the heart of Jerusalem and desecrates the Temple by setting up an altar to Zeus on which pigs are offered in sacrifice. While some Jews submit to the hellenisation process, many others, such as the Maccabean family, refuse. In 167 they issue a summons to like-minded Jews to join them in taking up arms against their oppressor. It is during these dangerous times that the procession of Israel's prophets is brought to a close with DANIEL, whose stories of Jewish heroism and apocalyptic visions afford much-needed comfort and encouragement to his hard-pressed compatriots.

Isaiah III, Haggai and Zechariah I
– supporting the homecomers

Isaiah III

Isaiah III, an anonymous figure like Isaiah II, worked among the exiles who took advantage of Cyrus' permission and returned home. So we are no longer in Babylon but in Jerusalem. The first wave of returnees is made up of Persian appointees, who want to make the territory a taxpaying province; priests who look forward to holding key positions in a restored Temple; opportunists who hope to make good pickings; and pious Jews who feel conscience-bound to return.[1] All will soon discover the harsh reality of living in a poverty-stricken land where they are made less than welcome. Isaiah III's aim is to encourage them not to lose heart.

Resemblances in style between Isaiah II and III are so marked that some scholars argue that a single author is responsible for chapters 40–66. A truer explanation might be that Isaiah III attempts to apply the teaching of Isaiah II to the situation facing the post-exilic community. Thus, while Isaiah II is centred on the hope of return, Isaiah III focuses on the renewal of those who have returned.

The first four chapters and the last four, a mishmash of praise and blame, surround the book's central core (chapters 60–62), the renewed glory of Jerusalem, fiancée of God.

Praise and blame (i)

God promises: "soon my salvation will come". A similar expression in Isaiah II offered hope to the exiles; here it exhorts those who have returned to do "what is right", in particular to keep the sabbath. A second promise assures entry into "my house of prayer" to two classes of people usually banned from the Temple: the non-Jew wishing to become a convert, and the eunuch (Deuteronomy 23:1-9), provided only that they keep the sabbath and hold fast to the covenant (56:1-8).

The leaders are mocked as "sentinels" that are "blind"; "silent dogs that cannot bark"; and "shepherds" with "no understanding" and filled "with strong drink". Pagan worship seems to be rampant; the language of adultery, whoredom, child-sacrifice, "stick[ing] out your tongue" (against the Lord in mockery?) is similar to that of the pre-exilic prophets in their attacks on

---

[1] V.H. Matthews, *Social World of the Hebrew Prophets* (Peabody, MA: Hendrickson, 2001), p. 150.

fertility cults. Perhaps Isaiah III simply "draws upon pre-exilic language to condemn sarcastically the worship of his own day",[2] which falls far short of what is expected.

There are words of consolation for the afflicted. "Build up, build up, prepare the way, remove every obstruction," cries the "one… whose name is Holy". This time "the way" is the path to salvation and is for "the humble" and "the contrite". The Lord hid from them because of their wickedness, but is still their Creator. He will heal them and they will know "peace". But "there is no peace… for the wicked"; the prophet is to lift up his voice "like a trumpet" and proclaim the people's sins. They come seeking the Lord "day after day", "as if they were a nation that practised righteousness", but their attitude towards the needy reveals their hypocrisy. There is no point in fasting from food if there is no fast from injustice. In fact on fast days they do business, wrangle, even resort to violence. That is not "a day acceptable to the Lord". The "fast that I [the Lord] choose" is one that includes caring for the needy – the oppressed, the hungry, the homeless, the naked (cf. Matthew 25). The importance of sabbath observance is stressed: with the exile at an end, some are tempted to put business interests before those of the Lord on "the holy day". Instead of simply repeating the third commandment, the prophet draws attention to the rewards that come to those who keep holy the sabbath day (56:9 – 58:14).

Lack of prosperity is due to the people's sins, "barriers between you and your God". Their hands are bloodstained, their lips soiled with lies. The plans they design are as dangerous as "adders' eggs" and as flimsy as "the spider's web"; with eagerness, "their feet run to evil". A communal confession of guilt acknowledges that sin is at the root of their troubles. The Hebrew words for "sin" in 59:12 – *pasha'* (to rebel), *chata'* (to miss a target) and *'avon* (to be crooked) – point to its far-reaching nature. But the Lord "saw that there was no one [to help]" and so he rose to their defence, girded, as he was at the Exodus and the conquest of Canaan, with a warrior's armour – breastplate, helmet and cloak – and the world trembles at his approach. "And he will come to Zion as Redeemer, to those… who turn from transgression" (59:15-21).

The new Jerusalem, fiancée of God

Chapter 60 begins with the exuberant cry: "Arise, shine, for your light has come." Zion is made radiant because the "glory" of the Lord is in her midst; and since "darkness shall cover the [rest of the] earth", the nations will be drawn towards Zion's light. The city thrills with joy at the sight of the peoples

[2] C. Stuhlmueller CP, "Deutero-Isaiah and Trito-Isaiah", in R.E. Brown, J.A. Fitzmyer and R.E. Murphy (eds), *The New Jerome Biblical Commentary* (London: G. Chapman, 1989), p. 344.

bringing home from exile her sons and daughters, bringing also, in caravans and ships, "the wealth of the nations". They come from Midian, to the far south, and Ephah, a tribe of Midian; from Sheba in south Arabia and from Tarshish, in southern Spain. Flocks are brought from Kedar and Nebaioth, renowned for their sheep and rams. It is even boldly suggested that the animals, destined for sacrifice, mount the altar of their own accord.[3] (The picture of the nations gathering with God's people and bringing gifts of gold and frankincense may have coloured the account of the Magi in Matthew 2:1-12; in the early Church it became part of the liturgy for the Epiphany.) When the city is renewed, foreigners will "build up your walls" and "their kings shall minister to you". The city's gates "shall always be open" for the endless procession of kings and nations bringing their wealth. Renewal of the city will be followed by renewal of the Temple, involving use of huge trees, "the glory of Lebanon". The descendants of Israel's former oppressors will worship in "the Zion of the Holy One of Israel". Restored Israel "shall suck the milk of nations" and will know that "I, the Lord, am your Saviour and your Redeemer." The transformation is a total reversal of the harsh conditions prevailing at the time of Isaiah III's ministry. A promise of peace and justice leads into an apocalyptic vision of the future when "the Lord will be your everlasting light" and there will be no need of sun or moon (60:1-22).

Using expressions from the second and third Servant Songs, Isaiah III declares that the Lord "has anointed" him with "the spirit" and sent him forth to bring "good news to the oppressed", bind up "the brokenhearted" and proclaim "liberty to the captives". The jubilee "year of the Lord's favour" has arrived; "the day of vengeance" (in the sense of restoration) has come, and all who mourn will be comforted. The prophet sees himself as fulfilling the role of the servant. (The greatest servant of all will one day apply these words to himself [Luke 4:17-21].) Israel will be a priestly people, "ministers of our God"; from the ashes of the old city a new Zion will emerge, and garlands, "oil of gladness" and songs of praise will replace signs of sadness and destruction. The people will rebuild "the ancient ruins" of Judah. Israel once knew suffering and shame; now the Lord will reward her with a "double portion" of "everlasting joy". The world will see that he has renewed his "everlasting covenant" with his people and will acknowledge them as "a people whom the Lord has blessed". And Israel rejoices like a bride, decking herself with jewels. God's saving work, like a seed, will cause plants of "righteousness and praise" to spring up (61:1-11).

---

[3] C. Westermann, *Isaiah 40–66* (Philadelphia: Westminster Press, 1969), p. 359.

Like the psalmist who could not forget Zion (Psalm 137), the prophet cannot "keep silent" about Jerusalem. In the Lord's name, he promises that all the nations will see her vindication, that she will be like "a crown of beauty" to the Lord, will receive a new name befitting her new status, will be called "My Delight Is in Her", and the land will be called "Married". Unfaithful Israel will again become the innocent spouse of the Lord, so that "as the bridegroom rejoices over the bride, so shall your God rejoice over you". Perhaps as encouragement to those who doubt, the prophet explains that "sentinels" posted on Jerusalem's walls will continually "remind the Lord" of the solemn oath he made. And so the people are urged to go out of the city gates, remove all obstacles and "prepare the way for" the exiles whose return is imminent. Finally, with renewed promises of the recompense the Lord brings, the people are assured that they are now "The Holy People", no longer the forsaken ones (62:1-12).

Praise and blame (ii)

Isaiah III has its oracles against the nations, similar to those in other prophets but without parallel in the violence of the language used, a violence that says more about the people than about the God it attempts to describe. For this community, like an alien in its own land and surrounded by injustice and violence, the fearsome picture of God crushing its enemies under foot was understandably a welcome one. "It is hard to speak about God in tender and winsome images when one finds life without much meaning and present existence as a terrible burden."[4] Like a sentry, the prophet enquires about the identity of the one who approaches him from the direction of Bozrah in Edom. The reply is the divine "It is I": the Lord comes "announcing vindication". The prophet asks why his garments are spattered with red like those of one treading a winepress. The horrific reply is that they are not wine stains but bloodstains from the trampling-down of enemies. Single-handed the Warrior Lord has won victory over Edom, Israel's traditional enemy, though here symbolising all her enemies. "Bozrah" means "vintage time" in Hebrew and Edom is linked with the Hebrew word for "red". Some commentators favour emending the text so that it runs: "Who is this that comes all in red, in crimson garments like a wine harvester?" This in turn has led to the application of the passage to the suffering of the Messiah[5] (63:1-6).

A long lament begins with grateful remembrance of the Lord's glorious deeds which flowed from "his steadfast love" (*chesed*): he called his people, saved and redeemed them, "lifted them up and carried them", despite their rebellions. They remember especially how he rescued them at the Exodus,

---

[4] Westermann, *Isaiah 40–66*, p. 374.
[5] *The New Jerusalem Bible*, ed. H. Wansbrough (London: Darton, Longman & Todd, 1985), p. 1287, note a.

but it all leads to an anguished cry – where is he now? – followed by an earnest appeal that the Lord will "look down from heaven", for without him they are lost. "Where", they want to know, "are your zeal and your might?" And where is "the yearning of your heart"? Twice he is appealed to as "our father" – a designation rare in the Old Testament because of its association with the physical fatherhood of the mythical gods – but he is their father in a way that even Abraham and Israel never could be. The prophet reproaches him for allowing the people to "harden [their] heart" against him, allowing their enemies to have "trampled down your sanctuary", and for leaving his people feeling no longer "called by your name".

He also begs the Lord to show himself even more spectacularly than at Sinai: tear open "the heavens and come down". But he admits that if the Lord "hid" himself and was "angry", they on their part have, through unfaithfulness, become "unclean" and their "righteous deeds are like a filthy cloth". Yet they still call upon him for help, appealing to him as "our Father". Acknowledging that they are his creatures, "the clay... the work of your hand", they beg him "not [to] remember iniquity forever" and end with the poignant plea: "After this... Will you keep silent?" (63:7 – 64:12).

The answer is not long in coming: the Lord "was ready to be sought" and "found", but they "did not seek me". He repeatedly assured them, "Here I am", holding out his arms to welcome them, but they chose to follow "their own devices" and provoke him by resorting to pagan cults as in pre-exilic days – burning incense in the high places, sitting "inside tombs" hoping to receive messages from the dead, and eating "swine's flesh", despite the law's explicit condemnation (Leviticus 11:7). And so the Lord's ominous words: "I will not keep silent, but I will repay."

However, while the unfaithful have earned condemnation, the Lord's servants are promised salvation. The whole nation is not to be compared to a bunch of grapes that is cast aside as worthless, for "there is a blessing [power of giving increase[6]] in it". "My servants" from Jacob (the northern kingdom) and from Judah will be a remnant that takes possession of the land from "the Valley of Achor", in the south-east, to the Plain of Sharon, in the north-west, and there they will live in peace. "But you", the Lord insists emphatically, you who "forsake the Lord", "forget my holy mountain" and worship the gods "Fortune" and "Destiny" – for you a different fate lies in store.

The next few verses tell of the good things to be enjoyed by "my servants", and the punishments to be meted out to the unfaithful, the repetition of

---

[6] Westermann, *Isaiah 40–66*, p. 404.

"but you" serving to underline the contrasting fates of the two groups. This simultaneous announcement of salvation and its opposite is reflected in the teaching of Jesus (cf. Luke 6:20-26), above all in his description of the Judgement in Matthew 25[7] (65:1-16).

And now a wonderful panorama opens up, as the Lord promises "to create new heavens and a new earth" and "to create Jerusalem as a joy, and its people as a delight", so that there will be no more weeping or cries of distress, no more premature deaths. The people may be painfully familiar with life in an occupied land; but now there is the promise that men's labours – building houses, sowing fields, caring for vineyards – like women's – bearing and rearing children – will not be in vain. The Lord will answer his people even "before they call" and (as in Isaiah 11) the animals will live in harmony (65:17-25).

The focus shifts as, at least according to the NRSV translation, the prophet engages in "the fiercest condemnation of Temple worship in the whole Bible",[8] apparently putting lawful acts of worship on a par with the most loathsome. However, another translation would give the meaning that in the Temple both lawful and loathsome are found side by side, and so it would be a plea for purification rather than a rejection of Temple worship; and also an insistence that the Lord's first home is not in the Temple but in heaven. The section ends with words of encouragement for those who are faithful to the Lord, while those who hate them "shall be put to shame" (66.1 5).

Then comes a song of ecstatic joy in the Lord's salvation, framed by two brief units. The first portrays the Lord as a warrior of divine justice (66:6): the "uproar" in the Temple is the sound of him "dealing retribution to his enemies". The second (66:14-17) presents him advancing with fire, chariots and sword to complete his victory, in particular punishing those who engage in pagan rites in secret gardens. The song compares the era of salvation to a wondrous birth in which labour pains and birth are simultaneous. "Who has ever heard of such a thing?" asks the prophet. But there are still those who think that the saving work, though begun, will never be accomplished. The Lord's answer takes the form of a rhetorical question: "Shall I open the womb and not deliver?" Again all are called to "Rejoice with Jerusalem", who is compared to a nursing mother holding her children close to her bosom. The prosperity she enjoys will be as extensive as the waters of a river in flood. Thus, "As a mother comforts her child so I [the Lord] will comfort you" (66:7-13).

---

[7] Westermann, *Isaiah 40–66*, p. 406.
[8] Stuhlmueller, "Trito-Isaiah", p. 348.

A gathering of "all nations and tongues" will witness "my glory". Not only will the exiles be brought home, but foreigners too will come to Jerusalem, even becoming "priests and... Levites". The text seems to suggest that some of them will be missionaries, bringing knowledge of the Lord to the people of far-away lands. The Lord promises that, in keeping with "the new heavens and the new earth", "all flesh shall come to worship before me". In frightening contrast, there will be unending punishment for his enemies. This black-and-white contrast between the fates of good and bad reflects the ultimate outcome of the cosmic struggle between good and evil (66:18-24).

We reach the end of the massive book of Isaiah, begun by Isaiah I of Jerusalem in the eighth century, enlarged two centuries later by Isaiah II during the dark days of the exile, and, after another half-century and the return of the first group of exiles, completed by Isaiah III. Five centuries later when the New Testament comes to be written it will contain more references and allusions to Isaiah than to any other Old Testament book, with the possible exception of the book of Psalms. Many passages from Isaiah I and II feature in the Advent and Christmas liturgies; the "Suffering Servant" passages of Isaiah II seem to anticipate vividly the redemptive sufferings and final triumph of Jesus; and the prophetic statement of chapter 61 (in Isaiah III) is quoted by Jesus himself in his first sermon at Nazareth (Luke 4:16-19). Little wonder that the magnificent book of Isaiah has been styled a "Fifth Gospel".

Haggai and Zechariah – urging Temple reconstruction

In 520, on their return from exile, Haggai and Zechariah began to preach; they encouraged the rebuilding of the Temple and saw their hopes fulfilled five years later. Little else is known about them. In the words of Ezra: "The elders of the Jews built and prospered, through the prophesying of the prophet Haggai and Zechariah" (Ezra 6:14).

Haggai
Exhortation to rebuild the Temple

Haggai mentions the Persian king, Darius – there is now no Jewish king – and his two representatives, Zerubbabel and Joshua, the leaders of the settler community in Jerusalem. Then he launches an attack on his fellow citizens. While agreeing in principle to the rebuilding of the Temple, they argue that "the time has not yet come". The time has not come, he retorts, for you to "live in your panelled houses, while this house lies in ruins". He points to the consequences of their procrastination: "Consider how you have fared" – failure of crops, lack of adequate clothing, inability to make money – all down to their neglect of the Temple. They must get timber for the rebuilding so that the Lord will receive his rightful glory and the relationship between him and his people will be restored. In the end Zerubbabel, Joshua and the people recognise the Lord's voice in the words of the prophet and respond by setting to work "on the house of the Lord of hosts" (1:1-15a).

The Temple's future glory

While the building is in progress, Haggai is commanded to invite the people to contrast the magnificent Temple of Solomon with the half-hearted reconstruction achieved since the exiles' return. The prophet also has words of encouragement: Zerubbabel, Joshua and the people are urged to "take courage" for "I [the Lord] am with you" in accordance with "the promise I made you when you came out of Egypt"; and "in a little while" the Lord will shake not only the universe – "the heavens and the earth and the sea and the dry land" – but all the nations, too, so that their treasures will fill the coffers of the Temple, and "the latter splendour of this house shall be greater than the former".

Haggai puts two questions to the priests: first, if a person carries "consecrated meat" (food blessed for sacrifice) through the Temple, would it sanctify all it touches? Second, if an unclean person passes through the Temple, does that person defile everything that is touched? In accordance with traditional ritual concepts of the sacred and the unclean, the priests reply negatively to the first question, positively to the second: holiness is not transferable but defilement is. The moral is: the "unclean" behaviour of the people makes their offerings, and the altar itself, "unclean" (or perhaps the unhallowed, makeshift altar, which was used before the rebuilding of the Temple, was regarded as impure and so as spreading its contagion to offerings and offerers alike[9]). However, while there were misfortunes in the past, "from this day on" – because the rebuilding is under way – "I will bless you", promises the Lord.

Finally, in an oracle for Zerubbabel, Haggai speaks of God shaking the elements and the nations, thereby robbing them of their power. "On that day, says the Lord of hosts, I will take you, O Zerubbabel... and make you like a signet ring." "In Jer 22:24 it [a signet ring] is used in an oracle of divine rejection of Jehoiachin; here it is used in an oracle of divine election of Jehoiachin's grandson."[10] Haggai's royal expectations for Zerubbabel may

---

[9] A. Cody OSB, "Haggai", in R.E. Brown, J.A. Fitzmyer and R.E. Murphy (eds), *The New Jerome Biblical Commentary* (London: G. Chapman, 1989), p. 351.
[10] Cody, "Haggai", p. 351.

not have been realised, but his promise about the renewed Temple and God's glory dwelling there was amply fulfilled (1:15b – 2:23).

> "The Bible gives principal credit for the rebuilding of the Temple to Haggai" and if this acknowledgement is correct "[his] oracles… represent one of the most important building proposals in history… Judaism survived the destruction of the second temple in 70 CE, but without the temple Judaism might not have lasted until that time."[11] And had Judaism not survived, there could not have been a Jewish child born in Bethlehem, whose name was Jesus.

Zechariah I

Like the book of Isaiah, that of Zechariah was not composed at one time or by one author. Zechariah I (chapters 1–8) is contemporaneous with Haggai, and is remarkable for its apocalyptic visions and its interest in messianism. Zechariah II dates from the late fourth century (see next chapter).

Introduction: summons to conversion

"The word of the Lord came to" Zechariah, "son of Berechiah", giving him the task of calling the people to return to the Lord: "Return to me, says the Lord of hosts, and I will return to you." They are not only to come back from exile and rebuild the Temple (a spatial return) but also to amend their ways (a moral return);[12] and are reminded that their ancestors did not listen to the prophets – and "where are they" now? In the end, they did learn the lesson and so there was hope for the future (1:1-6).

Night visions

A series of eight visions, extravagant in imagery, encourages the rebuilding of the Temple, while assuring the people that God, who appeared to abandon them in the exile, is still the Lord of history.

Vision 1: Zechariah sees "a man", apparently an angel, riding on a red horse. Through this angelic messenger in human form God communicates with the prophet. The scene is Eden-like, with the messenger seated "among the myrtle trees in the glen". His three fellow horsemen – on red, sorrel and white horses – who are sent by God to patrol the earth, report that "the whole earth remains at peace", and so there seems little chance of any change in Judah's

---

[11] J.M. Ward, *Thus Says the Lord* (Nashville: Abingdon Press, 1991), p. 262.
[12] A. Cody OSB, "Zechariah", in R.E. Brown, J.A. Fitzmyer and R.E. Murphy (eds), *The New Jerome Biblical Commentary* (London: G. Chapman, 1989), p. 354.

situation. The angel asks how long the Lord will continue to be "angry" with his people, as he has been for the past "seventy years" (a round figure for the period since the fall of Jerusalem). The prophet is told to proclaim that the Lord's anger is for the nations, despite their current peaceful condition; but his loving concern is for Judah, despite her present misfortunes. He has returned to Jerusalem "with compassion": "my house shall be built" and "my cities shall again overflow with prosperity" (1:7-17).

Vision 2 confirms the first: the angel explains that the "four horns" which now appear symbolise Israel's enemies, coming like wild beasts from every quarter. But four "blacksmiths" arrive on the scene and "strike down" these enemies (1:18-21).

Vision 3 introduces a surveyor who is about to measure Jerusalem, but the prophet tells him that "Jerusalem shall be inhabited like villages without [need of] walls" and will enjoy agricultural prosperity. The Lord "will be a wall of fire all around" to protect it and "the glory within it". Further oracles reinforce the message of the visions and call the exiles to flee home from Babylon, assuring them that their enemies will be destroyed, "many nations shall join themselves to the Lord" and "the Lord will inherit Judah as his portion" (2:1-13).

Vision 4: Zechariah sees Joshua, the high priest, standing apparently in the presence of the heavenly court with the angel and Satan in attendance. The latter, like a prosecuting barrister, draws attention to the high priest's vestments: his "filthy clothes" symbolise either his sins and those of the people or, more likely, the fact that during the exile certain rites of purification could not take place. But the Lord has him clothed in "festal apparel" and a "clean turban", promising that, so long as he is true to the covenant, he will have jurisdiction in the Temple and its courts. An unexpected reference is made to "my servant the Branch". It seems to refer to a messianic figure, as in Isaiah 11·1 where the image of the Branch looks towards an ideal Davidic ruler. It is more difficult to see the meaning of the "stone with seven facets" and the inscription engraved on it by the Lord, but clearly Zechariah wants his people to know that their apparent rejection by God is over, and that a day will come when they will live in freedom and enjoy mutual hospitality (3:1-10).

Vision 5: Awakened (or, perhaps, alerted) by the angel, Zechariah sees a golden "lampstand", surmounted by "a bowl" with "seven lamps" and flanked by "two olive trees". The lampstand may be a link with the golden lampstands that Moses and Solomon, respectively, placed in the tent of meeting and in the Temple, indicating that as God accompanied Moses through the desert and dwelt in Solomon's Temple, so the Lord is with his people still and wants the Temple to be restored so that his presence, represented by the lampstand, may dwell there. The messenger identifies Zerubbabel as the leader who, by the empowering of the Lord's spirit, will accomplish the task, though obstacles lie in his way like a "great mountain"; and, having "laid the foundation" of the Temple, "his hands shall also complete it": he will raise up "the top stone" to shouts of rejoicing even from those who mocked "the day of small things" (unpretentious beginnings). The angel explains that the seven "eyes" (facets) of the stone represent the eyes of the Lord ranging over the world; and the "two olive trees" with their "two golden pipes" are "the two anointed ones who stand by the Lord of the whole earth" – Joshua and Zerubbabel, appointed by the Lord to provide spiritual and political leadership (4:1-14).

Vision 6 moves from the leaders to the community: "a flying scroll" seeks out wrongdoers, exemplified by "everyone who steals" (those who harm their neighbour) and by "everyone who swears falsely" (those who betray God). Such evils violate the covenant and deserve the curse written upon the scroll (5:1-4).

Vision 7 makes it clear that "wickedness" is to be cleared out of the land. A woman hidden in a basket represents "wickedness" (perhaps because the Hebrew word for wickedness is feminine) and is borne away in her basket by "two [winged] women" and taken to "the land of Shinar" (Babylonia), where she will reign in the midst of the Babylonians (5:5-11).

Vision 8 has echoes of the first. It features four chariots, arriving from between two "mountains of bronze", each drawn by four red, black, white or dappled grey horses. The angel explains that the teams of horses with "the four winds" have, with God's approval, set out "to patrol [the four corners of] the earth", especially "the north country", homeland of the Babylonians. In an appendix, Zechariah is told to collect "silver and gold" from the returning exiles and fashion it into "a crown" for Joshua the high priest and also, apparently, for the civil ruler, the "Branch", who is to "build the temple of the Lord" and "shall bear royal honour". Finally, even "those who are far off" will actually take part in the rebuilding of the Temple; and so, says the prophet, "you shall know that the Lord of hosts has sent me" (6:1-15).

Israel's past history and messianic hope

A year after the visions and two years after the start of Temple restoration, a delegation arrives seeking guidance from the priests and prophets about certain ritual activities. Zechariah points to the self-centred nature of their laments and fasting (rites, presumably, for the anniversary day of the destruction of the former Temple), and reminds them that it was because their ancestors "refused to listen" to the Lord that they were exiled.

However, the final words of the Lord to the prophet are full of hope. They speak of his passionate concern ("great jealousy") for Zion and the returned exiles. He "will dwell in the midst of Jerusalem" and so the city and its inhabitants will be faithful and holy. Old and young alike (the two groups who would have found most difficulty in making the long trek back from Babylon) will now live in peace. It may seem impossible, but not to the Lord, who will bring back exiles "from the east country [Babylon] and the west country [Egypt]" to fill Jerusalem. Twice the people are challenged: "Let your hands be strong" – for the completion of the Temple. It will ensure that they enjoy "a sowing of peace", when vine and ground will be fruitful and the skies will water the earth. As the people were punished for unfaithfulness, so now they will experience God's goodness. They are urged to respect truthfulness, justice and love of neighbour, so badly neglected by their ancestors. And now an answer to the initial question raised by the delegation: the traditional times of fasting will henceforth be "cheerful festivals", and the people are to "love truth and peace".

Then, as a fitting end to the book, comes the promise that people will flock to Jerusalem from the ends of the earth because of the Lord's presence there; and Jews who dwell in the diaspora will pass the good news to others so that people of every nation will take hold of a Jewish neighbour by the sleeve, begging him: "Let us go with you, for we have heard that God is with you" (7:1 – 8:23).

But Jerusalem would one day have a glory that even Zechariah could never have imagined: in that city, God would be with us more intimately than ever before; Jerusalem would be for ever the holy city, so that even after more than two millennia innumerable pilgrims would flock there from the ends of the earth to honour the place made holy by the life, death and resurrection of the saviour of the world.

Zechariah II, Joel, Jonah and Malachi

– challenging the people

Little is known about these prophets beyond the fact that after the Temple was rebuilt they challenged the people to live up to the demands of the covenant.

Zechariah II

Judgement on Israel's enemies and the coming of Zion's king

An oracle of the Lord announces the destruction of hostile nations surrounding Judah; indeed, once they forsake their pagan practices, the Philistines will be assimilated among the Lord's people; nor will foreigners occupy Judah, because God dwells there. "Daughter Zion" is to "rejoice greatly" for a messianic king comes, "victorious" yet "humble and riding on a donkey"; and, with the implements of war banished, he will announce peace to the ends of the earth. (Matthew 21:5 and John 12:15 see a fulfilment of these words in Jesus' Palm Sunday entrance into Jerusalem.) The Lord will rescue the imprisoned, and, using the northern and southern kingdoms as bow and arrow, will destroy their enemies. The people will be led in a holy war to the accompaniment of heavenly portents. Despite graphic pictures of war's dire consequences, the outcome is pictured in terms of peace, pastoral plenty and people like "the jewels of a crown".

It is by relying not on "teraphim" (household idols) but on the Lord that they will get the rain needed for their flocks. Their leaders fail them, so that they are like a flock of wandering sheep. But then the image for the people changes to that of horses of war! The Lord is a warrior leading them to victory; leaders, with titles such as "cornerstone", "tent peg" and "battle bow", will emerge from their midst. The northern and southern kingdoms will be restored, while Israel's ancient enemies will be no more and a taunting song is raised against them (9:1 – 11:3).

Shepherd allegory and Jerusalem's deliverance

The prophet is appointed shepherd of God's flock, which is being exploited by bad rulers and due to be slaughtered; he takes two staffs, one tagged "Favour", the other "Unity". In "one month" (a short time) "the three shepherds" (the leaders) are disposed of. Meanwhile he breaks the two staffs, indicating on one hand annulment of the Lord's covenant with the people and on the other a total break between Judah and Israel. When the prophet decides to give up his shepherd role and seeks recompense for his efforts, he is offered a contemptuous "thirty shekels of silver", the price paid for a slave gored by an ox. The Sanhedrin, the false shepherds, appraised Jesus at the same "lordly price" (Matthew 26:14-15, though Matthew 27:9 attributes the words to Jeremiah!). In the prophet's case, as in Christ's (Matthew 27:5), the money is tossed into the Temple treasury. Finally the prophet is commanded to mimic an evil shepherd whom God will destroy for preying on the people (11:4-17).

A second oracle declares that when nations surround Jerusalem, they will be sent reeling like drunkards; they will damage themselves like men lifting a stone that is too heavy for them. The Lord will blind their horses' eyes but keep a "watchful eye" on his own people, enabling the "clans of Judah" to withstand those who try to approach Jerusalem via their territory. Meanwhile he will pour "a spirit of compassion and supplication" into his people and they will "look on the one whom they have pierced", mourning for him as for an only child – a passage interpreted in John 19:37 as fulfilled in the piercing of Christ. The mourning, which will involve the family of David (civil rulers), Nathan (prophets), Levi (Levites) and Shimei (priests), will be like the lamentation for the storm-god on the plain of Megiddo, and in response "a fountain shall be opened" to cleanse the people from their sins; idols will be removed, as will false prophets, who wear the distinctive "hairy mantle" and often bear self-inflicted "wounds". A song of the sword tells how the shepherd will be killed and the sheep scattered (a text applied to the flight of the apostles in Matthew 26:31). The people will be sifted and those who come through successfully will acknowledge the Lord as their God, as he will acknowledge them as his people (12:1 – 13:9).

The Lord reigns

The final chapter promises a "day… for the Lord", when "all the nations" will assault Jerusalem. Her citizens will face dreadful trials and, after half of them have been deported, the Lord will intervene as divine warrior. At his appearance on the Mount of Olives, the mount will divide – like the parting of the Exodus waters – and the valley thus created will be a protected escape route.

After this eschatological trial, a new age begins in which there is no more cold or darkness, and a river, the sign of God's blessing, flows out from Jerusalem; and God becomes "king over all the earth" and Jerusalem, as befits a royal city, is raised aloft, never again to be destroyed. As for enemies, they are visited by a plague that throws them into such panic that they slay one another. Those who survive will worship the Lord in his Temple in the annual "festival of booths" (Tabernacles), while any nation not represented at the feast will suffer from lack of rain. Finally, the sacredness proper to the Temple spreads outwards so that there is no distinction between holy and profane: the most mundane objects such as horses' bells and cooking pots will be as holy as the sacred Temple vessels, and all the people – not just the priests and Levites – will be involved in sacred cooking. And – perhaps an attack on current practices – all buying and selling will be prohibited in the Temple (14:1-21).

Joel
A plague of locusts and a call to repentance

There is much scholarly debate about the date of Joel, though general agreement that it is post-exilic. The only biographical information is that Joel was "son of Pethuel". After "the word of the Lord" comes to him, in the late fifth or early fourth century, he interprets the devastation caused by a plague of locusts as a symbol of "the day of the Lord". The locusts – 1:4 indicates either four species or four stages in their growth – are so numerous that they are like "a nation", with the fangs of wild animals. The "wine-drinkers", "the priests" and the "farmers" are called, respectively, to "wake up", "lament" (like a young bride over her dead husband) and "be dismayed". The priests, having failed to offer Temple sacrifices, are urged to don sackcloth, "sanctify a fast" and summon "a solemn assembly" of "all the inhabitants of the land". The lament begins ominously: "the day of the Lord is near" and with it shortages of food, loss of crops, starvation of animals and severe drought.

The sound of "the trumpet" (*shofar* or ram's horn) makes the people tremble; it announces a locust plague that is like an invading army, so that what before its arrival was a "garden of Eden" is in its wake "a desolate wilderness"; its noise is like the "rumbling of chariots" or the crackling of burning stubble; unswervingly, it mounts the city walls and the earth seems to quake. "The day of the Lord is... terrible indeed." The Lord calls the people to "return to me" with fasting, weeping and mourning. The return, encouraged by the recital of God's mercy and steadfast love, must be sincere: hearts, not merely clothing, must be rent and, in the end, all depends upon God's sovereign will. Again the *shofar* sounds: all – from the aged to children at the breast, even bride and bridegroom – are to express repentance at "a solemn assembly". The Gentiles will not be left wondering: "Where is their God?" for the Lord will respond magnificently, giving fruitfulness of every kind and a sure supply of rain. The end of the plague and alleviation of the drought will be proof that he is still "in the midst of Israel" (1:1 – 2:27).

Day of the Lord: consequences for Israel and the nations

The presence of the Lord will lead to a re-creation, which will affect "all flesh" and be characterised by an outpouring of the Spirit (as "in the beginning" [Genesis 1:1-2]); there will be portents in the sky, outdoing those associated with the locusts; and "everyone who calls on the Lord shall be saved". Now the day of the Lord becomes one of rejoicing for Israel, but of judgement for Israel's enemies. (On Pentecost Day, Peter sees Joel's words fulfilled in the outpouring of the Holy Spirit and the empowering of the disciples to prophesy and be witnesses of the resurrection [Acts 2:17-21].) When he restores Judah, "my people and my heritage", the Lord will summon all the nations to "the valley of Jehoshaphat". Joel probably has in mind the meaning of the name ("God judges") rather than a specific place. Traditional enemies will experience the tragedies they imposed on Judah – plunder and the selling of people into slavery. The valley is a valley not only of judgement but also of war: the prophetic call for peace – "beat your swords into ploughshares…" (Isaiah 2:4 and Micah 4:3) – is reversed and made into a battle cry. The putting in of the sickle and the treading of the winepress become images for the punishment meted out by the Lord. Portents fill the sky and the roar of the Lord's voice is heard, and, finally, comes a promise of abundant food, destruction of enemies and the lasting presence of the Lord in Zion (2:28 – 3:21).

Jonah

"Jonah son of Amittai" is the eponymous hero of this book, written in about the fifth century BC but set in eighth-century Nineveh. Though a fictional character, Jonah is the only prophet "with whom Jesus identifies himself"[1] (cf. Matthew 12:38-41; Luke 11:29-32). Commissioned to preach to the Ninevites, Jonah takes ship in the opposite direction, "to Tarshish" in Spain. When a storm blows up, he confesses that he is responsible and agrees to be thrown overboard. The storm subsides and "the Lord [provides] a large fish to swallow up Jonah" (chapter 1). After "three days and three nights" his prayer is heard and the sea monster regurgitates him on shore at the very place from which he set out (chapter 2). The divine call is repeated and this time Jonah obeys. In Nineveh he proclaims his one-sentence message (only five words in Hebrew): "Forty days more, and Nineveh shall be overthrown!" Then, the unimaginable happens: the godless Ninevites repent, they fast – even the animals wear sackcloth! (chapter 3).

Jonah knows how God will react: the slightest sign of repentance, and mercy will be shown to the Ninevites – which is not at all what Jonah wants.

---

[1] P. Murray OP, *A Journey with Jonah* (Dublin: Columba Press, 2000), p. 9.

God provides "a bush" to shelter the sulking prophet from the blazing sun. When, later, it is removed, Jonah is angry; he wants to die. God replies: "You are concerned about the bush… should I not be concerned about Nineveh, that great city in which there are more than a hundred and twenty thousand persons…?" (chapter 4).

We are not told how Jonah responded, but the message of the book is clear: God is inclusive, longing to show mercy to all people; when they turn back to God, God turns back to them. This "doctrine marks one of the peaks of the Old Testament… We are on the threshold of the New Testament." [2] The book of Jonah, "the most profoundly Christian book of all the books in the Hebrew bible",[3] still challenges us today.

Malachi

This may be the work of an anonymous prophet since the Hebrew *Mal'achi* means "My i.e. God's messenger". Because of its dialectic character, it has been likened to a running debate, consisting of a statement, an objection and then a rebuttal. It consists of six oracles and two appendices.

Six oracles

Oracle 1 speaks of the Lord's special love for his people. The disturbing assertion, "I have loved Jacob, but… hated Esau", is a powerful way of declaring his preferential love for Israel, though his power is not restricted to Israel's borders (1:1-5).

Oracle 2: Israel's special relationship brings special responsibilities. As "a son honours his father, and servants their master", so the Lord expects respect from his people, especially the priests, yet they offer blemished animals in sacrifice. They ought to try presenting such gifts to their Persian governor! It would be better if the Temple doors were shut altogether. Their behaviour compares unfavourably with that of "the nations" who make God "a pure offering". (From early Christian times 1:11 has been applied to the Eucharist, offered "from the rising of the sun to its setting".) Priests, who ought to have "walked with me in integrity and uprightness", have forfeited the promises given by covenant to the Levitical priesthood (1:6 – 2:9).

---

[2] *The New Jerusalem Bible*, ed. H. Wansbrough (London: Darton, Longman & Todd, 1985), p. 1189.
[3] Murray, *Journey with Jonah*, p. 10.

Oracle 3: Since all have "one father" – for the second time (see 1:6) God is spoken of as "father" – faithfulness should mark all human relationships. Those who marry foreigners, children of "a foreign god", are unfaithful to God and to their fellow Israelites and run the risk of being drawn into idol worship. No husband should be "faithless to the wife of his youth" because God, the guarantor of their union, hates divorce (2:10-16).

Oracle 4 is a response to those who, seeing the prosperity of the wicked, cynically enquire: "Where is the God of justice?" God will "suddenly come to his temple"; a "messenger" will prepare his way. (In Matthew 11:10 Christ applies these words to John the Baptist, who prepared the way for his coming.) The day of his coming will be a day of purification, especially for the priests (2:17 – 3:5).

Oracle 5 declares that it is because the Lord is changeless that the people "have not perished", despite their persistent unfaithfulness. Even now he begs them to return: in particular to stop "robbing" him by cheating in their tithe-giving. Then he will pour out on them "an overflowing blessing" (3:6-12).

Oracle 6: There are cynics among the people, but there are also "those who revered the Lord", and the coming "messenger" will distinguish between the groups: "a book of remembrance" will be kept and the Lord assures the righteous, "They shall be mine… my special possession" (3:13-18).

Two appendices[4]

On the day of the Lord the wicked will experience oven-like burning, but those who fear the Lord will experience the healing rays of the "the sun of righteousness" and will be renewed. (Handel took his image of the refiner's fire, in the *Messiah*, from Malachi.)

After a plea that they remember the laws that Moses brought them from Mount Horeb (Sinai), the people are promised that "the prophet Elijah" will return before the day of the Lord. Jesus will explain that the Baptist's ministry is the fulfilment of the promise (Matthew 17:10-13).

> Thus the final words of the last of the prophetical books (in the Hebrew Bible the prophets are arranged in a different order) look towards the coming of Christ, and serve as a reminder that the prophets – and indeed the whole of the Old Testament – are preparing the way of the Lord.

---

[4] Chapter 4 in the NRSV appears in the Hebrew as 3:19-24.

12 Daniel
– heroic deeds and apocalyptic visions

This book, dating from the time of the Maccabean uprisings (167–164 BC), aimed at sustaining the Jews in the persecution of the tyrant Antiochus IV Epiphanes. Part, possibly all, of it was originally in Aramaic. Because it was compiled after the closure of the official list of Prophets, it is placed in the Hebrew Bible among "the Writings", but in Greek and Latin versions it is found among "the Prophets", where some additional material is also added. In chapter 3 there is the Prayer of Azariah and the Song of the Three Young Men, and at the end of the book two additional chapters recall further popular stories about Daniel: his rescue of Susanna from the wicked elders (chapter 13) and his defeat of the Babylonian idols Bel and the Dragon (chapter 14).

The book falls into two sections: the first (chapters 1–6) consists of stories about Daniel – the book's hero rather than its author – and his three young friends who were taken to the Babylonian court during the exile in the reign of Nebuchadnezzar but remained faithful to the Law; the second (chapters 7–12) consists of apocalyptic visions.

Heroic deeds

These legendary stories – like historical novels with a religious message – encourage the Jews to stand firm by reminding them of the power of the Lord, who rescues his faithful ones. Thus, Daniel and his companions, brought to "Shinar" (Babylon) and given Babylonian names, courageously adhere to Jewish dietary laws and flourish. In chapter 2 Daniel (his companions appear only incidentally) interprets the king's dream, which his own wise men could not, by "reading" the four sections of a huge statue as successive empires (Babylonian, Median, Persian and Greek), and the destruction of the statue by "a kingdom that shall never be destroyed" as an intervention by God and his Messiah and the establishment of God's eternal kingdom. ("This is the intervention which Jesus... declares imminent in Mt 4:17, 23" and which will achieve its final realisation with the return of Christ in glory.[1]) Nebuchadnezzar, deeply impressed, exclaims, "Your God is God of gods."

In chapter 3, when Daniel's companions refuse to bow before an idol erected by the king, they are thrown into a fiery furnace but, after earnest prayers, the three young men emerge unscathed and Nebuchadnezzar declares his faith in their God.

---

[1] *The New Jerusalem Bible*, ed. H. Wansbrough (London: Darton, Longman & Todd, 1985), p. 1615, note f.

Daniel interprets another ominous dream in chapter 4, explaining that while Nebuchadnezzar has brought blessings to his people, yet because of his refusal to accept the power of the Lord he will experience a period of insanity and only after repenting will he be restored.

Chapter 5 tells how, during a banquet hosted by Belshazzar (a later successor of Nebuchadnezzar), Daniel interprets the message written on the wall by a mysterious hand: the days of the kingdom are numbered, its sins weighed and it will be divided.

Chapter 6 records how in the reign of Darius envious courtiers report Daniel for continuing to pray, despite a royal edict that forbids it. Thrown into the lions' den, David is miraculously preserved and the king issues a decree "that in all my royal dominion people should tremble… before the God of Daniel".

Apocalyptic visions

These chapters are characterised by visions, bizarre symbolism, interpreting angels, emphasis on the final days of persecution and/or of the world. Daniel's first dream presents four beasts emerging from the sea; like the statue in chapter 2, they represent successive kingdoms that have oppressed Israel. The horns stand for particular kings and the "little" horn, with "eyes like human eyes" and "a mouth speaking arrogantly", for Antiochus. A judgement scene follows: the "Ancient One" (the Lord), whose white hair and shining clothes symbolise wisdom and greatness, takes his seat upon a fiery throne and "the books" of judgement are opened. The fearful kingdoms are destroyed or allowed to linger on for "a season and a time" (a short period). Then "one like a human being", coming in the clouds (as opposed to the beast-like creatures emerging from the sea), approaches the Lord and receives sovereign dominion over all peoples and nations. "One like a human being" (or "son of man") has a first meaning of "man"; in Daniel 7 it becomes a symbol of faithful Israel (see "the holy ones" of 7:22); later it was interpreted to mean an individual Redeemer figure; and finally "Son of Man", occurring more than seventy times in the synoptic Gospels, seems to be Jesus' preferred way of referring to himself.

Chapter 8 takes us to the royal residence at Susa, where Daniel has a vision, echoing that of chapter 7. A he-goat (Alexander and his empire) overcomes a ram with two horns (Medes and Persians). Finally, the "little horn", Antiochus, appears, his power reaching "the beautiful land" (Palestine) and "the host of heaven" (Hebrew wordplay apparently referring to the statue with which Antiochus profaned the Temple). The angel Gabriel interprets the vision for Daniel.

Jeremiah proclaimed that the exile would last seventy years (Jeremiah 25:11), but the reinstatement of God's favour, which was supposed to follow, had not occurred though several centuries had passed. In chapter 9, in response to Daniel's fasting and moving prayer, Gabriel explains that Jeremiah's "seventy years" in fact means seventy weeks of years. Thus, the small persecuted Jewish community is reassured that the long night is now almost over.

The final three chapters (10–12) "foretell" events occurring between the exile and the death of Antiochus (in fact most of them had already happened). A dazzling angel promises Daniel "understanding" by offering him a brief account of the Persian empire and then of Alexander the Great.

The story of various kings (not always identifiable with certainty) culminates in the "warrior king", Alexander, whose kingdom was divided "toward the four winds", that is, between his four generals. Later it fell into the hands of two dynasties – the Ptolemies in Egypt ("the king of the south") and the Seleucids in Syria ("the king of the north"). In their struggle for control of Palestine, the Seleucids were the victors, and from their number arose "a contemptible person", Antiochus IV. He usurps the throne, acts "as he pleases", considers himself "greater than any god", even Israel's God, plunders the Temple and persecutes God's people. His wretched death is predicted and, though the placing of it "between the sea and the beautiful holy mountain" (the Mediterranean and Jerusalem) is inaccurate – he died in Persia – his death was indeed lonely and miserable.

A passage, which includes the first clear expression of Old Testament belief in resurrection of the dead, explains how, despite "a time of anguish", all those whose names are "written in the book" of life "shall awake... to everlasting life". In a way typical of apocalyptic writing, Daniel is told to keep the revelation secret until the appropriate time. Then, in what is probably a later addition, Daniel overhears two heavenly beings announce that the distress will last "a time, two times, and half a time" (three and a half years), though the period is revised to 1,290 days in 12:11-12! The final sentence is again an expression of belief in the resurrection of the dead.

The book of Daniel features largely in the liturgy; with its references to eternal life, the Son of Man and the eternal kingdom of God, it serves as another reminder of the part played by prophets in preparing the way for the Lord. In the words of an eminent theologian: "how could Jesus be acknowledged without the promises made, the visions painted, the expectations prompted by Israel's prophets?"[2]

[2] A.E. Lewis, *Between Cross and Resurrection* (Grand Rapids, MI: Eerdmans Publishing Co., 2003), p. 113.

THE KINGDOMS OF ISRAEL AND JUDAH

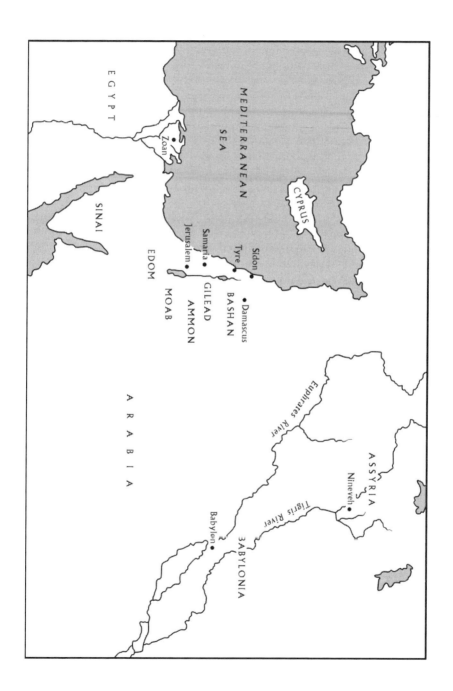